THE SEA

THE SEA

THE SEA

ANGELO S. RAPPOPORT

SENATE

The Sea – Myths & Legends

First published in 1928 as *Superstitions of Sailors* by Stanley
Paul & Co, London

This edition published in 1995 by Senate, an imprint of
Studio Editions Ltd, Princess House, 50 Eastcastle Street,
London W1N 7AP, England

ISBN 1 85958 149 8

Printed and bound in Guernsey by
The Guernsey Press Co. Ltd

CONTENTS

		PAGE
	PREFACE	9
CHAPTER		
I.	THE ORIGIN OF THE SEA	15
II.	WATERSPOUTS, PHOSPHORESCENCE, ST. ELMO'S LIGHT	45
III.	WINDS AND STORMS	63
IV.	FOLK-TALES OF WINDS AND STORMS	95
V.	ENCHANTED ISLANDS AND ROCKS	125
VI.	THE WORLD BENEATH THE WAVES	141
VII.	THE DENIZENS OF THE DEEP (MERMEN, MERMAIDS, KELPIES AND WATERSPRITES)	157
VIII.	FOLK-TALES OF MERMEN AND MERMAIDS	183
IX.	SEA-MONSTERS	205
X.	PHANTOM SHIPS AND APPARITIONS	221
XI.	OMENS AND CEREMONIES	253
XII.	SUPERSTITIONS OF SAILORS IN ENGLISH LITERATURE	273
	BIBLIOGRAPHY	281
	INDEX	283

LIST OF ILLUSTRATIONS

THE SEA . . . . *Frontispiece*

FACING PAGE

THE ODYSSEY 16

SAILORS RETURNING FROM A SEA VOYAGE . . . 56

FISHERMEN, BY TROYON 88

MERMAID 160

MERMEN & MERMAIDS FOLLOWING A VESSEL . . 176

SEA MONSTER 208

THE PHANTOM SHIP 224

THE FISHERMAN'S FAMILY 256

PREFACE

WHAT is the origin of the superstitious beliefs to which the seafaring man is even to-day still clinging? It may be attributed to three sources, viz. : Firstly, the interpretation and explanation of numerous phenomena actually observed, but the cause of which the early mariner was still ignorant of ; secondly, the inclination of man to look for the causes of events in mystical depths and supernatural reasons ; and thirdly, the love of travellers to exaggerate and to tell adventures which in reality they had never experienced.

Numerous stories told by early mariners were subsequently handed down from generation to generation and formed a portion, if not the bulk, of early mythologies. Such, for instance, is the journey of the Argonauts and the legend of the floating rocks which destroy ships. The entire Odyssey is practically nothing else than a collection of sea-stories current among the Greeks at the time of Homer and collected by the latter. The stories of Circe changing into swine the companions of Ulysses and of the sirens who allure men by their songs are either due to the imagination of some sailor, or are the account of happenings to some mariner in a distant land. The raging sea opening its mouth to swallow the craft will have given rise to the legend of the Scylla and Charybdis.

For the seaman the sea is not inanimate nature, but some living creature which breathes and feels and is conscious of its existence. In the noise of the waves the Icelander hears the groan of a dying man, while to the lively imaginative Scotsman the foam-crested waves are so many dogs running in front of their master. The Frenchman calls the shimmering crest on the greenish water—*moutons*.

The ignorance of natural phenomena resulted in exaggeration and gave rise to peculiar beliefs and superstitions. Anything strange has a hold on the imagination of man. The beliefs of pagan antiquity were of course modified according to the changes in religious creeds, but many illusions and delusions prevailed all through the Middle Ages. In our own age habits and customs, old beliefs and superstitions, are fast fading away and perishing, yet many of them still hold their ground, and sailors, naïve and childlike, tenaciously cling to them.

I have made an effort in the present work to introduce the reader to the numerous superstitions, past and present, of the seafaring community and have described the various beliefs still current. I have also included a number of folk-tales, drawn from numerous sources, dealing with the sea, wind and weather, mermen and mermaids. I have everywhere indicated the original sources of the legends and tales collected and have added a bibliography. I hope, therefore, that the reader will peruse the following chapters with interest and to some advantage, while the student of Folklore may also find therein points to interest him.

ANGELO S. RAPPOPORT.

THE ORIGIN OF THE SEA

THE CREATOR OF THE SEA

Over all the face of Earth
Main ocean flowed, not idle, but, with warm
Prolific humour softening all her globe,
Fermented the great mother to conceive,
Satiate with genial moisture ; when God said,
" Be gathered now, ye waters under heaven,
Into one place, and let dry land appear ! "
Immediately the mountains huge appear
Emergent, and their broad bare backs up heave
Into the clouds ; their tops ascend the sky.
So high as heaved the tumid hills, so low
Down sunk a hollow bottom broad and steep,
Capacious bed of waters. Thither they
Hasted with glad precipitance, uprolled,
As drops on dust englobing, from the dry :
Part rise in crystal wall, or ridge direct,
For haste ; such flight the great commend impressed
On the swift floods. As armies at the call
Of trumpet (for of armies thou hast heard)
Troop to the standard, so the watery throng,
Wave rolling after wave, where way they found—
If steep, with torrent rapture, if through plain,
Soft-ebbing, nor withstood them rock or hill ;
But they, or underground, or circuit wide
With serpent error wandering, found their way,
And on the washy ooze deep channels wore :
Easy, ere God had bid the ground be dry,
All but within those banks where rivers now
Stream, and perpetual draw their humid train.
The city land Earth, and the great receptacle
Of congregated Waters He called Seas.

MILTON.

CHAPTER I

THE ORIGIN OF THE SEA

The mystery of the sea—Appeals to the credulity of man—The wet origin of the Universe—The *Laws of Manu*—The story of Creation in the *Mahabharata*—The earliest cosmogonies—Homage paid to the sea—The origin of the Sea in the *Mahabharata*—The virgin Luonnatar—A Sumatra legend—The salty taste of sea-water—A Moslem legend—The arrogance of the sea—A Jewish legend—The sea and the sand—The magic mill grinding salt—The mill song—Menia and Fenia, the two female slaves—The legend of the two brothers—The flitch of bacon and the wonderful quern—The skipper and the sea—Virtues attributed to the saltiness of sea-water—A drenching with sea-water—Superstitions in Scotland—Folk-medicine—Sea-water as a purgative—Bathing when the tide is rising—healing virtues of sea-water—The waves—The keys of St. Peter—The cry of drowned men—The number of the waves—The three waves—The cabin-boy and the two witches—The waves and the unfleshed sword—The ninth wave—The mother-wave—The tide—Superstitions of early mariners—The traditions of Japan—Scandinavian Sagas—The princess who had one hundred children—The monster of the deep—The tide and childbirth—The influence of the tide in Scotland—Customs in Sweden and Scotland—Neck, Neck, needle-thief—Stones thrown into the water.

THE sea, that marvel of creation, immense and mysterious, silent or stormy, smooth or agitated, troubled and treacherous, has from time immemorial appealed to the imagination of primitive man. Ignorance, irrational fear, and a desire to propitiate the occult and unknown powers are generally the cause of man's superstitious beliefs. No wonder, therefore, that humanity in its early childhood should have been struck with fear and awe by that wide expanse hiding in its deep both dangers and treasures. The sea appealed to the credulity of man and exercised his imagination, and all those whose occupations compelled them to spend their lives upon the water wondered and thought about the origin of the sea and all the phenomena connected with it.

The capricious element, inspiring both horror and confidence, was peopled with imaginary beings, while the riddle of its very origin gave rise to numerous theories and superstitious beliefs. What is that wide expanse of water and whence has it come ? asked not only the ancient cosmogonists but also the mariners who had to perform a sea-voyage.

The knowledge of meteorological principles and a better acquaintance with nautical science has, of course, done a great deal towards abolishing the many delusions prevailing with regard to the watery element, but the ignorance among sailors and fisher-men is still very great, and seafaring men even to-day cling to numerous superstitions. Sailors generally believe that the sea existed from the beginning of time and that it had, in any case, been created before the earth. In this respect the belief of mariners coincides with the majority of theories expressed in ancient cosmogonies. The theory of

THE ODYSSEY
by Ingres

the wet origin of the Universe is found in the cosmogonies of Egypt and India, of Assyria and Greece, and the Greek philosopher Thales taught that the sea was the origin of all things. The *Avesta*, or the sacred book of Zoroaster, and the *Kalevala* of the Finns, both relate that water was the first or one of the first elements.

In the elaborate story of Creation, found in the *Laws of Manu*, "the eponymous ancestor of mankind and the first lawgiver," it is related that in the beginning the Self-Existent Being desired to create living creatures. He first created the waters, which he called " Narah," and then a seed ; he flung the seed into the waters, and it became a golden egg which had the splendour of the sun. From the egg came forth Brahma, Father of All. Because Brahma came forth from the waters, and they were his first home, he is called Narayana. In the *Mahabharata* the sage Markandeya is informed by the Lord of All that the waters called " Nara " were his home and therefore his name was Narayana. The Egyptian Sun God Ra similarly rose from the primordial waters as the sun-egg. According to the Aztecs the entire creation and even the gods themselves, the earth, the sun, and the stars, lay concealed in the fathomless abyss.[1]

We thus see that the earliest cosmogonics attributed priority to water. To primitive man the

[1] Brinton, *Myths of the New World*, p. 129.

watery element appeared both as a friend and as an enemy, a devouring monster at one time and a god fighting on his side at another. No wonder that the ancient mariners who spent their lives on the sea should have looked upon the ocean with feelings of both awe and horror. They firmly believed, and this belief is still extant to-day among the seafaring community, that the primeval ocean had been rolling its waves through a timeless night.

The sea, according to the beliefs of many, is the daughter of the Gods. Hesiod relates that earth gave birth first to Uranus, crowned by the stars, and then to Pontus, and subsequently uniting itself to Uranus produced the bottomless ocean. In Oceania it is believed that Tane married to Taaroa gave birth to the sea and the wind, while the Polynesians say that all things created issued from their respective mothers, and the sea, too, had one. According to other traditions the sea is not the daughter of the Gods, but a divinity itself or a part of it, a belief which explains the reason why certain nations paid homage to and worshipped the sea. Macrobius[1] says that the heaven constituted the head of Serapis, while the sea was its belly. In Scandinavian tradition the origin of the sea is explained as follows: In the beginning there was neither sand nor sea, but only Guinunga-gap, the abyss of abysses. Thereupon the sons of Bur killed the giant Ymer,

---

[1] *Saturnales,* I, XX.

placed his body in the midst of Guinunga-gap and thus made earth. From his blood became the ocean and his bones constituted the mountains.[1]

In the *Mahabharata* the origin of the sea is related as follows : The sea having been dried up by the Saint Agastya, its bed remained empty for several thousands of years. At a certain moment, however, fixed by Brahma, the pious Bhahgirata obtained the favour of Civa and of the celestial river Ganga. The latter consented to descend from heaven and falling upon the luxurious hair of Civa, poured into the empty bed which it filled.

The sea, according to many ancient traditions contained the germs of everything, and the earth, submerged in the sea, awaited the moment when the creative fiat made it emerge above the waters. In the *Kalevala* the virgin Luonnotar came down from heaven and plunged into the sea, which made her fruitful. She swum in the waves for seven centuries, but one day she lifted her knee above the waters and the eagle deposited there his eggs. On the third day, Luonnotar having lowered her knee, the eggs fell into the sea. From their lower portion came the earth and from the upper portion the sublime heaven. The white of the eggs constituted the moon and the yolk the sun.

In Sumatra the following legend is related : In the days when nothing but water existed, one of the

---

[1] See Thorpe, *Northern Mythology*, Vol. I, Sect. I.

most famous Sumatran gods, Batara Gourou, had a daughter, Puta Orla Boulang, who desired to come down from heaven. She came down upon a white owl and her father, so as to enable his daughter to find a firmer footing, sent down from heaven the mountain Bakarra to which the entire earth adhered. Batara Gourou also sent down his son Layand Mandi commanding him to bind the hands and feet of Nagapagoha, the serpent who carried the earth upon its head and had hurled it once into the sea, so as to prevent the monster from making the earth disappear again in the waters.

The Salty Taste of Sea-Water

British sailors pretend that at the bottom of the sea the water is not at all salty, and when the fish is not catching it is because the water on that spot is not salty.[1] Drummond-Hay relates a story current among the Berber tribes of Morocco, which explains the cause of the salty taste of sea-water. In the beginning God had created the sea and in His goodness had made the water sweet. In their arrogance, however, the waters flooded the earth so that men and all other creatures, except the fish, perished. To punish the sea God sent an insect which swallowed up the sea so that its bed became dry. The sea thereupon repented, and God com-

[1] Mélusine, II, col. 200.

manded the insect to spit out the water it had swallowed. The tiny creature obeyed, but the water of the sea henceforth remained salty, having acquired this taste in the stomach of the insect.[1]

There is a similar legend of Moslem origin which accounts for the salty taste of the sea-water : In the first days of the world God created the sea, but remembering man, His masterwork of creation, He put a limit to the power of the watery element. " I command thee," said the Creator to the sea, " to respect that portion of the earth on which plants and flowers will grow to delight man. I have granted unto thee many privileges, for thy surface will reflect the azure of the skies and thy roaring waves will be the echo of my thundering voice." The sea promised to respect that portion of the earth which God had placed beyond its sway. Soon, however, the sea, proud and arrogant, forgot its promises and defied the Eternal. Discharging its roaring waves, it flooded the earth, and man was on the point of perishing. Then God interfered and decided to teach the arrogant waters a lesson in humility. He sent a swarm of insects who swallowed up the sea. From the inside of the tiny creatures the rebel loudly proclaimed the power of the Eternal and repented of its arrogance. The sea was forgiven, but its waters lost for ever their sweet taste.[2]

[1] Drummond-Hay, 1844, p. 304 ; Mélusine, II, col. 283.
[2] *Boletin folklorisco expanol*, Jan. 1885.

The arrogance of the sea is also the motif of a
Jewish legend, although no reference is made there
to the salty taste of the sea-water. On the third day
of creation, runs the legend, the earth was as flat
as a plain, the waters covering the entire surface of
the earth. At the word of the Creator the waters
gathered and were rolled into the valleys, and the
hills and mountains appeared. The waters then
became proud and arrogant, rose tumultuously to
a great height, covered the face of the earth, and
threatened to overrun and drown the terrestrial
globe. But the Creator rebuked the arrogant
waters, subduing them and placing them beneath
the hollow of His feet, making the sand the boundary
and fence of the sea. And when the mighty waters
saw the sand-grains, how small and insignificant
they were, they laughed at them and mocked them.

" We are not afraid of you," they said, " for the
smallest wave will destroy you and swallow you
up."

The sand-grains, appointed to fight against the
waves of the sea, were frightened, but the biggest
of the sand-grains said :

" My brothers, do not be afraid. We are power-
less and insignificant as long as we are separate,
and the slightest breeze can blow us away. If, however, we stick together, we are a great power and
able to oppose the inrush of the arrogant waters."

And ever since the waters recede and return to

their place when they see the sand-grains united into one compact mass.[1]

A legend current among the sailors of the coast of Ille et Vilaine explains the salty taste of the sea-water as follows : Once upon a time there lived a sorcerer who had invented a mill that could grind anything that the sorcerer commanded it to. The mill would only stop when the inventor pronounced a certain formula. One day a mariner heard of this wonderful mill and stole it. When he reached the open seas, the mariner commanded the mill to grind a quantity of salt which he required for the codfish he was out to catch. Soon the vessel was full of salt, but, alas, the mariner, ignorant of the magic formula, had no power to stop the mill in its work. On and on the mill continued to grind large quantities of salt so that the vessel and the mill sank to the bottom of the sea under the heavy weight. The mill is still continuing to grind the salt, and hence the salty taste of the sea-water.[2]

In *Northern Mythology* we read the following tale, which is called " The Mill Song."

King Frodi once paid a visit to King Fiölnir in Sweden, and there bought two female slaves, called Fenia and Menia, who were both large and strong. At that time there were found in Denmark two millstones so large that no one was able to drag

[1] *Pirke de Rabbi Eliezer*, Chap. III ; Rappoport, *Myth and Legend*, Vol. I, p. 14.
[2] Mélusine, II, col. 198.

them. These millstones had the property that they produced whatever the grinder wished for. The mill was called Grótti. Hengi-Kiaptr was the name of him who gave the mill to Frodi. King Frodi caused the slaves to be led to the millstones, and ordered them to grind gold, and peace, and prosperity to Frodi, giving them no longer rest or sleep than while the cuckoo was silent or a song might be sung. It is said that they then sung the song called Gróttasavngr, and before they left off that they ground an army against Frodi ; so that in the same night there came a sea-king called Mysing, who slew Frodi and took great spoil. Mysing took with him the mill Grótti, together with Fenia and Menia, and ordered them to grind salt. At midnight they asked Mysing whether he had salt enough ? He bade them go on grinding. They had ground but a little more when the ship sank. There was afterwards a whirlpool in the ocean, where the water falls into the eye of the millstone, and thence the sea became salt.[1]

A Norse tale explaining the reason why the sea is salt runs as follows :

Once upon a time there were two brothers, one rich and the other poor. One Christmas eve the poor hadn't as much as a crumb of bread in the house and so he went to his brother to ask him for something to keep Christmas with. The brother was

[1] Thorpe, l.c., I, p. 207.

not very generous and rather reluctant to offer help.

" If you will do what I ask you," he said, " I will give you a flitch of bacon."

" I will do anything you will ask me to," replied the poor brother.

" All right," said the rich brother, " here is the flitch of bacon and now go straight to Hell ! "

The poor brother looked surprised.

" Well," retorted the rich man, " have you not promised to do what I asked you. I am asking you to go straight to Hell and you must keep your word."

" What I have given my word to do," said the poor man, " I must stick to." So he took the flitch of bacon and set off.

He walked the whole day until he met a very old man with a long white beard who was hewing wood for the Christmas fire.

" Good even," said the man with the flitch of bacon.

" The same to you," replied the old man ; " whither are you going so late ? "

" O ! I am going to Hell, but don't know the right way."

" You have come to the right place," replied the old man, " for this *is* Hell. When you get inside they will all want to buy your flitch of bacon, for meat is rather scarce in Hell. Now don't you sell it unless you get the hand quern which stands behind the door. When you come out I will teach you how to handle the quern, for it is good to grind almost anything."

The man with the flitch thanked his informant and knocked at the devil's door. When he got in all the devils, great and small, swarmed up to him like ants round an anthill and all were anxious to buy the flitch of bacon, each trying to outbid the other.

" If I sell it at all," said the possessor of the flitch, " I will have for it the quern behind the door yonder." The devil did not like to part with the quern and haggled with the man for a long time, but as the latter stuck to what he had said he at last received the quern for his flitch of bacon. When he got out into the yard the friendly woodcutter showed him how to handle it. He thanked the old man and went off home as quickly as he could. The clock had struck twelve on Christmas eve before he reached his own door.

" Wherever have you been so late," asked his wife. " I have been waiting for you hour after hour, and I have not so much as two sticks to lay together under the Christmas fire."

" Oh," said her husband, " I could not get back before. " I had to go a long way for one thing and another ; but now you shall see what you shall see."

Thereupon he put the quern upon the table and

bade it grind lights, and a tablecloth and food and drink. To the amazement of his wife the quern did as it had been bidden. Soon the pair had everything they wanted and they were happy and content. The quern ground drink and dainties enough to last until Twelfth Day.

On the third day he asked all his friends and kin to a great festival. His brother also came and was very jealous when he saw all that was on the table.

" Where, in Hell's name," he asked, " have you got all this wealth ? "

The owner of the quern would not at first let the cat out of the bag, but, at last, when he had had a drop too much, he produced the quern and made it grind all sorts of things. When the rich brother saw the wonderful quern he set his heart on it and coaxed his brother so long until the latter consented to sell it to him for three hundred dollars. He told him how to make the quern grind the things he wanted but never told him how to make it stop.

As soon as the rich brother got the quern he bade it grind herring and broth for dinner, and the quern obeyed. Soon, however, not only the dishes and all the tubs were full of herring and broth, but the kitchen floor was covered, and all the efforts of the rich brother to stop the quern proved futile. The quern went on grinding and the owner was at a loss what to do. He rushed out of the house and set off down the road with the stream of herring and broth at his heels, roaring like a veritable waterfall. He came to his brother's house and begged him for God's sake to take back the quern. The brother, however, would not hear of taking the quern back until the other had paid him another hundred dollars.

The poor brother thus got both the money and the quern and he soon became a rich man and set up a farmhouse much finer than the one in which his brother lived. He bade the quern grind gold and he covered his house with plates of gold. As the house stood by the seaside, it gleamed and glistened far away over the sea. All those who sailed by put ashore to see the rich man and the wonderful quern.

One day a skipper came along who wanted to see the quern.

" Could it grind salt ? " he asked.

" I should think it could," replied the owner of the quern. " It can grind anything."

" If I could have that quern," thought the skipper, " I would be rid of the long risky voyages across stormy seas for a lading of salt. I must have that quern."

He begged and prayed so hard and so long until the rich man at last consented to sell his wonderful quern to the skipper for a good many thousands of dollars.

The skipper now got off with the quern on his

back, brought it on board his ship and quickly set sail. When he had sailed a good way off, he brought the quern on deck and said :

" Grind salt, and grind both good and fast."

The quern obeyed and began to grind salt that it poured out like water. When the skipper had got the ship full of salt, he wished to stop the quern, but however much he tried, his efforts like those of the rich brother proved of no avail. The quern kept on grinding and the heap of salt grew so high that the ship at last sunk down.

The quern lies at the bottom of the sea, and grinds away at this very day, and that is why the sea is salt.[1]

Another story explaining the cause why the waters of the sea are salty runs as follows :

Once upon a time there was a skipper who fell in love with one of his neighbours and ultimately married her. The captain thereupon undertook a long sea-journey and during his absence a mighty lord dwelling in the neighbourhood fell in love with his wife and carried her off by force to his castle. When the captain returned home from his sea-journey and learned the sad news, he was greatly distressed. Unable to compel the mighty lord to restore his wife to him, he sought consola-tion in another long sea-journey which lasted several

---

[1] Asbjornsen and Moe, *Norske Folkeeventry* ; see Sir G. W. Dasent, *Popular Tales from the Norse*, Edinburgh, 1859.

years. On his return home he heard that the sea had suddenly submerged the castle and that all the inmates had been drowned. His wife alone had escaped. The captain rejoined his beloved wife and they lived happily together.

" How was it," asked the captain, " that you were not drowned like the others ? "

" The sea," replied the woman, " seems to have done its best to spare me. It never touched the place where I had taken refuge, and as soon as all the inmates of the castle had been drowned, the waters suddenly retired."

" Since the sea has spared you," said the captain, " I must go and thank it for its kindness." He went to the seashore and heartily thanked the sea for its kind action, inviting it to follow him. The sea did not reply, but it silently followed the captain who took it to a country full of salt mines. That is the reason, why the sea is now salty.[1]

Sailors attribute many virtues to the saltiness of sea-water. Thus on the Breton coast they pretend that sea-water renders the members of the body pliant and supple, while in Poitou and in Gironde sea-water is said not to wet the body. Sailors on the coasts of Finistère and Morbihan are convinced that one never catches a cold by bathing in sea-water. If a drenching with sea-water would have such dangerous effects as a drenching with fresh

[1] Sébillot, *Legéndes et Croyances*, I, pp. 75–76.

water, no sailor or fisherman would venture to embark, as they are constantly exposed to a drenching. On the contrary, people who have caught a cold in the head quickly get rid of it by being wetted by sea-water. There is a general belief in Scotland that a plunge in sea-water never has such effects as a drenching with fresh water. Bathing in the sea is believed to be more wholesome than in fresh water.[1] The best way to get warm, when it is cold, they say at Tréguier, is to have a dip in the sea.

Many virtues are ascribed to the saltiness of sea-water in folk-medicine. In Brittany sailors believe that the best treatment for a cold in the head is to drink a glass of sea-water in the morning and in the evening. In Poitou people believe that sea-water cures bronchitis, and a glass of sea-water drunk in the morning is an excellent remedy for a sore throat. In Tréguier sea-water is used as a purgative on account of the salt it contains. When drinking the water in spring or in the autumn it is customary to blow on it first so as to expel the impurities and also to spill some of it on the ground. The water should be taken at the moment of the ebbing tide. In Scotland it was quite common, not many years ago, to use sea-water as a purgative. When the water was to be put to this purpose, it had to be drunk in the morning before taking any food. As large a draught as possible was drunk. Bathing

[1] Gregor, *Folklore Journal*, 1884, p. 356.

is most commonly done when the tide is rising, from the belief that the water is strongest and has most effect at that time. Sea-water is much used as a lotion in cases of local inflammation, weakness, or stiffness of a joint, and spine disease.[1]

Sea-water, they believe in Brittany, is an excellent remedy for eye-disease. One has only to bathe the eyes with sea-water seven or eight times by holding the head a little inclined for a quarter of an hour. The operation should best be performed in the morning before sunrise and in the evening after sunset. In Brittany sea-water is said to be a splendid remedy for erysipelas, and it is considered to be efficacious for wounds which should be washed with the ebbing tide.

In the neighbourhood of St. Malo sea-water is supposed to possess a healing virtue for diseases of pigs.[2]

THE WAVES

Numerous beliefs are connected with the waves and their origin. According to some of them the waves are the result of a voluntary movement and agitation of the sea which is considered as an animate being. The nations of antiquity believed that Gods presided over the waves. Thus among the Greeks and the Latins it was Poseidon who produced the

[1] *Folklore Journal*, 1884, p. 356.
[2] Mélusine, II, col. 200.

waves and made them subside. The ancient
Scandinavians, for whom the waves were the
daughters of the Goddess Rana, believed that the
movements of the sea were produced by the Gods
or the genii. Thor hurled the waves against the
cliffs and produced the whirl in the hollow of the
rocks.[1]

In Portugal a belief is current according to which
the waves are the result of a celestial punishment.
St. Peter is holding two keys in his hand, one
golden and the other black. The waters of the sea
are in constant motion as a punishment ordained
by Divinity, but they never leave their bed, thanks
to the power the key of St. Peter has been endowed
with. On the Channel coast sailors and mariners
believe that the waves are due to the action of the
wind. According to a tradition current in the
neighbourhood of St. Malo the sorcerer who once
lost his magic mill plunges from time to time into
the water in order to recover his property, and it
is this plunge which produces the waves.[2] The
sound and noise of the waves are believed to foretell
certain events. Thus on the coast of Cork, when
the waves are producing an extraordinary roaring
noise it is taken as predicting the death of a great
man. In Brittany the belief exists that the tumultuous sound of the tossing waves is nothing else

---

[1] See Thorpe, I, p. 72.
[2] Mélusine, II, p. 198.

but the cry of the numerous drowned men who are restless and agitated as long as their bodies have not yet been found and buried in consecrated ground.[1] A similar belief exists in Scotland.[2] Certain waves are supposed to warn people of the danger threatening them. A great number of sailors are firmly convinced that certain birds of the high seas, such as the albatross and the petrel, lay their eggs upon the waves. This belief is also to be met with in the East.

THE NUMBER OF WAVES

A good many sailors attribute particular virtues and powers to the third, the ninth, and the tenth waves. They believe that after a time a certain regularity is established in the movement of the waves. In every three waves, they say in Brittany, one is more powerful than the others. It is that wave that produces the loudest roar. This belief is also shared in Finistère. In Scotland they believe that in a tempest there are always three strong and violent waves, while the fourth wave is comparatively the weakest and the least dangerous. This succession of waves is called the *rote of waves*.[3]

There are numerous legends and sailors' stories clustering round the waves. Witches are said to take the shape of waves in order to cause vessels

---

[1] Mélusine, II, p. 254.
[2] See Gregor, *Folklore Journal*, 1885.
[3] Gregor, *Folklore Journal*, 1885, p. 56.

to sink and to drown the people on board against whom they have a grudge.

The following story, entitled " Three Waves," is a good example. One night when the cabin-boy was lying on deck as if he were asleep, he suddenly saw two women appear on deck as if they had fallen down from the sky. They carried the vessel through the air to an olive-wood and then, after having disappeared for a little while, came back, brought the vessel to its starting-point and made it fast. Thereupon one of the women said to her companions that all those who will board the vessel will be drowned because in spite of the calm weather, she will raise three terrible waves, the first of milk, the second of tears, and the third of blood.

" There is only one remedy for the ship to escape its destiny," said the elder woman to the younger, " and that is to throw a harpoon into the midst of the third wave, the wave of blood, for that wave will be myself. I will be hiding beneath the waves invisible to all, but the harpoon touching the wave will pierce my heart."

The cabin-boy having told his experience to the captain, the latter ordered a sailor to throw the harpoon into the midst of the third wave. The sailor executed the order and a moan was suddenly heard, while the wave was split in twain and running towards the shore covered with a bloody foam. The vessel caught a lot of fish on that day, for the charm had been broken. When the captain returned home he found his wife ill in bed. She died soon afterwards, cursing her husband, for it was she and her daughter who had hitherto bewitched the craft.

A similar legend is related by Koehler :[1]

One day three men from an island in the north of Friesland embarked upon the same vessel. During their absence their wives practised sorcery and, distrusting their husbands, followed them in different disguises. Thus they learned of the latter's infidelity and made up their minds to be revenged and to sink the vessel. They were conversing among themselves on deck, believing everybody to be on shore, but the cabin-boy overheard them. They said that they had nothing to fear as their plan could only be frustrated if an unblemished and chaste boy attacked them with an unfleshed sword. The cabin-boy procured himself a new sword and, a tempest having arisen, he began to walk on deck to windward. Soon he saw three waves as high as towers and white as snow. He presented his sword and immediately the waves fell down and the sword was dyed red. When the vessel landed at Hamburg, the captain and his two companions learned that their wives had suddenly fallen ill, precisely on the night of the three waves.

A Welsh tradition attributes to the ninth wave a particular virtue and reminds us of the Scandinavian

[1] Mélusine, II, col. 200–201.

belief in the nine waves, daughters of the sea. The ninth wave is supposed to be the most powerful and to reach the shore before the other waves.[1] The superstition attaching to the power of the ninth wave is reflected in Celtic literature.

English sailors make the sign of the cross when they see the ninth wave come. On the coasts of the Charente-Inférieure some sailors believe that the tenth wave is the most powerful. This superstition existed already in antiquity and continued until quite recently.

In the Shetland Islands there is a tradition that before the introduction of the mariners compass old fishermen could find the land in a dense fog through their knowledge of the mother-wave (da-moder-die) or some wave-motion that indicates the direction of the land. Occult virtue is attributed to the third wave, more than to the first, although the reason is known only to the initiated. Karl Blind, writing on the subject, says : " Three is a sacred number from the most ancient times. Trinities of Gods are to be met with in classic, as well as in Germanic and other mythologies. Such are : Odin, Wili and We ; Odin, Hoenir, and Odin, Thor, Freya and Freyr." These trilogies are endless. It is therefore easy to account for the virtue of the third wavelet ; three being so hallowed a number.[2]

---

[1] Mélusine, II, p. 202.
[2] *Gentleman's Magaz.*, 1882, Vol. CCLII, p. 364.

THE TIDE

Many beliefs and superstitions are current among sailors in connection with the tide, its cause and its influence.

Thus certain sailors believe that the tide is due to the motion of the earth. They compare the phenomenon to a vase full of water. If one inclines the vase the water will go to one side, while the opposite side of the vase will remain dry. Sailors on the channel coast are generally convinced that it is the moon which commands the sea, and that the tides are caused by its action in connection with that of the sun and the stars. In Brittany sailors believe that low tide is due to the fact that the sea had retired into the air. The sea thus remained for six hours upon earth. The sea, say the sailors on the channel coast, cannot rise in one place without diminishing on the other side. Certain sailors pretend to prove this assertion by the following explanation : If one throws an object into the sea at low tide the water will carry it to a distant shore. This, they argue, is evident proof that when the tide is low here it rises at another place.

The phenomenon of the tide was almost unknown to the ancient Greeks, their navigation being limited to the Mediterranean Sea where the tides are almost insignificant. Had the Greeks had occasion to notice the tides they would no doubt have had special Gods in their Pantheon whose business it would have been to preside at this particular natural phenomenon. When the fleet of Alexander the Great remained on dry land in the Indian Ocean, the soldiers were frightened, and so also were nearly two centuries later the soldiers of Cæsar when they beheld the ebbing tide. But the writers of antiquity were acquainted with the phenomenon of the tide and endeavoured to explain it. *Pomponius Mela*[1] enumerates several such explanations, among them that given by Plato. According to this philosopher the universe is a living being, and the tide is due either to the fact of its drawing in or exhaling its breath. The tide, said Plato, could also be attributed to the numerous caverns and hollows at the bottom of the sea which in turn swallowed and threw back the water. Apollonius pretended that the tide was brought about by the submarine winds which were housed in the caverns. It was a movement similar to the drawing in and exhaling of breath.[2]

In the traditions of Japan the tides were supposed to be the work of malevolent deities, Yaco-Magatshi and Oho-Magatshi, whose numerous progeny are known as the Maga-Kami, or the genii of error. When Ho-hodemino, married to the daughter of the god of the sea, desired to return to earth, his

---

[1] Vol. III, Chap. I.
[2] Philostrates, *Life of Apollonius*, IX, p. 2.

father-in-law made him a present of two stones, one for the rising and the other for the ebbing tide. " If thy brother wishes to retain thee," said the God of the sea, " throw the first stone into the sea and the waters will immediately submerge the earth. Thou wilt only have to throw the second stone into the waters to make them resume their former limits."[1]

In the Scandinavian Sagas we are told that the gods themselves produce the tide. Thor, plunging a tube into the depth of the Ocean, raises the water with his powerful breath and then lets it fall again.[2] Chinese philosophers explained the phenomenon of the tide as follows : One day there was a princess who had one hundred children, fifty of them living on the seashore and fifty in the mountains. From these children issued two powerful nations who are constantly waging war one with the other. When the inhabitants of the seashore are victorious and put the enemy to flight they cause the incoming tide, but when they suffer defeat and retreat from the hills to the seashore they produce the ebbing tide.

According to many beliefs, some of which are still prevalent, the tide is caused by a monster of the deep. The sea, some sailors pretend, is a living being, and like a living being it breathes. Thus in

---

[1] Metchnikoff, *L'Empire Japonais*, p. 210.
[2] Réclus, I, p. 118.

the Shetland Islands the belief prevailed that in the depths of the sea there dwelt a sea-monster whose breath was the cause of the tide.[1]

The tide has given rise to a number of other beliefs and superstitions. Thus sailors in Lower Brittany believe that the rising tide is full of a poison which it deposits on the beach. It is therefore advisable to use the water only with the ebbing tide. At this moment only the sea-water is pure and more salty, the outgoing tide having swept away the poison together with the froth.

The phenomenon of the tide has puzzled the minds of the peoples of antiquity and is still puzzling the simple folks of modern times. Those who witness the rising and ebbing tide daily are bound to attribute to this phenomenon all sorts of supernatural influence. Like the stars, who are believed to be the arbiters of human destiny, the tide is responsible for many an event. Thus in Brittany the belief prevails that children are usually born with the rising tide, while in Tréguier, on the contrary, it is a common belief that women give birth with the ebbing tide. The Bretons maintain that boys are born with the incoming tide, while girls see the light of day with the outgoing tide. In Brittany people believe that a sick man gets better with the incoming tide, but that his strength diminishes with the ebb. The belief that the tide and

[1] *Gentleman's Magazine*, 1882, pp. 461-2.

ebb have an influence upon the destiny of man was current in antiquity. Thus Aristotle said that no animal expired except with the ebbing tide. This belief was current all through the Middle Ages and for a long time was shared even by medical practitioners in England, France, and Holland.

The superstition that people only die with the ebbing tide existed all through the Middle Ages. Many people even now cling to the belief that no one dies with the rising tide. In Boulogne the expression *s'en aller avec la mareé* is synonymous with *to die*. The superstition also exists in Portugal and in America. It is alluded to by Shakespeare in *Henry V*, II, p. 3.

In Brittany sailors maintain that if a dog drinks sea-water and swallows the foam produced by the tide he goes mad. On the other hand, with the ebbing tide, a mad dog has no strength to bite. In Brittany, and in the neighbourhood, people wait for the outgoing tide to kill pigs, as the bacon is then much better. In Lower Brittany pigs are killed with the incoming tide, sows with the outgoing.

In Scotland the influence of the tide has given rise to many beliefs and superstitions. Thus the health-giving power of the tide is asserted not only in the case of human beings, but also of animals. Lugworms are much used as bait for fish. When they are not wanted immediately they must be kept alive. It is believed that this can be done only by keeping them among water drawn when the tide is rising. If the water is changed daily they may be preserved alive for eight days or more, whereas, if they are put into water taken from an ebbing tide, they die within a short time. Sea-water is altogether much used in cases of local inflammation, weakness or stiffness of a joint, and spine disease. The water, however, must always be drawn when the tide is rising.[1]

There is a popular belief in Sweden that when bathing in the sea, a person should cast into it, close by him, a fire-steel, a knife, or the like, to prevent any monster from hurting him. The steel, or whatever it may be, may be taken out again. Formerly a fire-steel or a pair of scissors, was laid on the cradle of a child, until it was christened. Having thus propitiated the Neck or mischievous Spirit, or rather neutralized his pernicious propensitives, it was not unusual while bathing to address him scoffingly in the following words: " Neck, Neck, needle-thief, thou art on the land, but I am in the water." On quitting the water, the person took the steel again, saying : " Neck, Neck, needle-thief, I am on land, and thou art in the water."[2]

This reminds us of a custom which existed in Scotland to throw into the water before entering it

---

[1] Gregor, *Folklore Journal*, 1884, p. 356.
[2] Thorpe, l.c., II, p. 82–83.

three stones of different sizes, beginning with the largest. White stones, if they could be found, were preferred. Words were repeated, as the stones were pitched in, but the informant of the writer could not recall them.[1]

[1] *Folklore Journal,* 1884, p. 356.

WATERSPOUTS, PHOSPHORESCENCE AND
ST. ELMO'S LIGHT

They that go down to the sea in ships,
That do business in great waters,
These see the works of the Lord,
And his wonders in the deep.
For he commandeth and raiseth the stormy wind,
Which lifteth up the waves thereof,
They mount up to the heaven, they go down again to the depths :
Their soul melteth away because of trouble.
They reel to and fro, and stagger like a drunken man,
And are at their wit's end.
Then they cry unto the Lord in their trouble,
And he bringeth them out of their distresses.
He maketh the storm a calm,
So that the waves thereof are still.
Then are they glad because they be quiet ;
So he bringeth them unto the haven where they would be.

PSALM 107.

CHAPTER II

WATERSPOUTS, PHOSPHORESCENCE AND
ST. ELMO'S LIGHT

Waterspouts—Superstitions connected with waterspouts—Origin
of—The monstrous serpents—Long-tailed dragons—A monster drawing up the waves—Seamen's terror of waterspouts—
The discharge of artillery—A knife with a black handle—Its
efficacy in Ireland—Quotations from the Gospel of St. John—
Phosphorescence—The *brasi*—Small fishes turned blue—
The souls of the drowned suffering in hell—The devil of the
sea—The jet of flames—The lantern carried by the sorcerer—
The burning cask of the devil—The precious stones in the
water-demon's garden—The jewels of the nymphs—The
eyes of the Leviathan—The lightning among the masts—
Castor and Pollux—Superstitions of sailors—Feu St. Elme—
Jack with a lantern—Corbie's aunt—St. Elmo, the patron
saint of seamen—*Cuerpo santo*—The crew of Columbus—The
voyage of Magellan—An interesting scene described in a sea-
novel—The soul of a poor mariner—The drops from the wax
taper—Jack Hurry—Souls in pain—A malevolent spirit—
The origin of the light of St. Elmo—The saint and the sea-
captain—The miracle—St. Elmo and Saint Christopher—
The lantern upon the rock.

WATERSPOUTS, on account of their
surprising effect, their sudden appearance and extraordinary shape, could not
fail to strike the imagination of sailors : all sorts
of causes are attributed to them not only in ancient,
but also in modern times. In Brittany there exists
a belief that waterspouts are sent by God for the
purpose of feeding the clouds. The latter, instead of
bursting and sending down the rain, ascend into the

air. A similar belief also exists in Greece.[1] Breton
sailors believe that waterspouts sweep everything
they find in their way. A vessel surrounded by waterspouts runs a great risk of foundering. It is sure
to sink if it has not been baptized.[2]

The Arab mariners of the Middle Ages attributed
waterspouts to a dragon. In the sea there are
monstrous serpents called *tannin,* and during the
winter, when the clouds are touching the surface
of the water, the tannin rises up and enters the
cloud. Seized by the sudden cold, the serpent
remains imprisoned in the cloud. When the wind
begins to blow over the water the clouds rise up,
carrying with them the tannin. When the vapours
have been dissipated, the tannin, there being nothing
any longer to hold it, falls down either upon land or
upon the sea. Sailors and captains have often
maintained that they had perceived the monster
passing over their heads in the air.

The Japanese believe that the waterspouts which
they see so often off their coasts are long-tailed
dragons, flying up into the air with a swift and
violent motion ; they are called *tatsmaki,* or spouting
dragons.[3] The Chinese believed that waterspouts
are caused by the ascent and descent of the dragon.
Fishermen and sailors catch an occasional glimpse
of the dragon as he descends to the water and

---

[1] Pitré, *Météorologie,* p. 45.

[2] Mélusine, II, col. 206.

[3] Kaempfer, *Japan ;* see Pinkerton, *Voyages,* Vol. VII, p. 684.

ascends from it, but the monster is never seen head and tail at once.[1] In the Mediaeval Chronicle of John of Brompton we read of a wonder which happens about once a month in the Gulf of Satalia, on the Pamphylian Coast. A black dragon appears in the clouds, and while his tail remains fixed in the sky, he lets down his head into the waves. He draws up the waves to him with such avidity that even a laden ship would be taken up on high. In order to avoid the danger the crews have to shout and beat boards so as to frighten and drive away the dragon.[2]

Sailors of antiquity have always regarded the waterspouts with great terror. As the appearance was generally accompanied with flashes of lightning and a sulphurous smell, the Greeks called them *frester*, signifying a fiery fluid. The danger was very great to mariners of ancient times, as the wind blowing in sudden gusts in the vicinity of waterspouts, from all points of the compass, was sufficient to capsize small vessels carrying much sail. A practice exists even to-day to discharge artillery in order to accelerate the fall of the moving columns. This practice of modern times existed already in former days. Then, however, the idea was to frighten the dragon who was supposed to be responsible for the waterspouts by the noise and to

[1] See Doolittle, *Chinese*, Vol. II, p. 265.
[2] See Chron. John Brompton.

induce the monster to run away. The Arabs
indeed attributed the origin of waterspouts to the
movement of dragons and serpents who are either
rising up from the depths of the ocean or are suddenly swooping down from the air upon the wide
expanse of the sea and are raising up the waters with
their tongues.

Another means, considered to be efficacious
against waterspouts, consisted in a mariner holding
in his hand a knife with a black handle, and after
reading the Gospel of St. John, cutting the air with
his knife athwart the waterspout, as if he
would really cut it.[1] A knife with a *black* handle
is, by the way, even now considered in Ireland
as very efficacious against malevolent spirits,
fairies and nymphs who attack the wanderer at
night.

The efficacy of the quotations from the Scriptures
were considered as efficacious by the mariners who
accompanied Columbus. When faced by waterspouts the sailors were terrified at their appearance
and, despairing of all human means to avert them,
followed the practice of repeating passages from the
Gospel of St. John. The waterspouts passed close
to the ships without injuring them, and the sailors
naturally attributed their escape to the powerful
remedy they had employed.

[1] See Thévénot, *Travels in the Levant.*

PHOSPHORESCENCE

Sailors on the Channel coast say that the *brasi*, as they call the phosphorescence of the sea, is produced by small fishes turned blue by the effect of the stars. They also say that a sort of phosphorus rises from the bottom of the sea when fierce winds are blowing. In Brittany sailors say that when the sea is phosphorescent a muffled plaintive sound is often heard. Old fishermen pretend that it proceeds from the souls of the drowned suffering in hell, the fire of which is at that moment blazing.

The phosphorescence of the sea, according to the belief of Breton sailors, is also produced by an enormous fish living at the bottom of the sea and making war upon the small fishes. The big fish is called the devil of the sea and in order to destroy his enemies he throws out through his nostrils a jet of flames which sets the surface of the water on fire.

On the Channel coast there is a tradition that the phosphorescence of the sea is due to the lantern carried by the sorcerer who is searching for his magic handmill.[1] According to a tradition current in Pomerania, the phosphorescence of the sea is produced by the burning cask of tar on which the devil is navigating upon the water. When the sea is phosphorescent and the fishes are rising to the

[1] See Mélusine, Vol. II, col. 198.

water's surface, sailors in Brittany say that a fire is burning in the water which the fishes are making an effort to escape from.

Breton sailors also believe that the water-demon possesses a magnificent garden at the bottom of the sea where the souls of the pious drowned are dwelling. This garden is ornamented with diamonds and precious stones shining in the darkness. It is this glamour which makes the water appear as if set on fire.[1]

A good many sailors pretend that the phosphorescence of the sea is produced by the jewels of the nymphs and sirens, which only shine in the water. There is a legend attributing the phosphorescence of the sea to the burning vessel built by Satan and destroyed by St. Elmo.

The *Talmud* relates that one day two Rabbis went on a sea voyage and suddenly perceived a brilliant light on the waters. One of the Rabbis, quoting the words from Job xli, 18, explained that this light no doubt proceeded from the eyes of the Leviathan.[2]

The appearance of lightning amidst the masts gave rise to a curious superstition among mariners. A brilliant light is said to play amidst the masts and spars and cordage of the *Flying Dutchman*, but long before Falkenberg had stabbed his brother's bride,

[1] Sébillot, l.c., Vol. II, p. 111.
[2] Baba Bathra, 74b.

this light was known to seamen and caused them to
wonder. A single flame was considered to be an
evil omen, while two flames indicated a successful
voyage. The single flame was known as Helena,
and the two were termed Castor and Pollux. From
the times of antiquity, all through the Middle Ages
and down to modern times, the superstitious
sailor, unable to explain the meteorological reasons
of this mysterious light, has looked upon it with a
mixture of mistrust, joy, fear, and wonder. With a
childish naïveté and wondering speculation the
seaman of all times had tried to explain the phenomenon so mysterious to his simple mind. The
flames were to him auguries of either success or
misfortune, indicating storm, shipwreck, and even
death, or a very prosperous and successful journey.

The *Lettres Ediflantes* quote a curious incident.
One day the seamen of Malacca beheld the light of
St. Elmo during a storm and immediately began
to insult the supposed demon, for to them the
light was a demon. " Why have you come on board
our vessel ? " they cried. " Our goods do not belong
to you, they have been paid for. Go to the pirates
who have acquired their goods by pillage. Your
father is a thief and your mother and sisters are
dissolute women." Thereupon they armed themselves with sticks and began to shout, not daring,
however, to climb up the mast.[1]

[1] See *Folklore Journal,* 1883, p. 396.

This light was called Dioscures or Helena by the
Greeks, Castor and Pollux in Latin, and is known
as the feu St. Elme or feu St. Erme in French, and
as St. Elmo's light or " Jack with a lantern " in
English. St. Helen's fire, and Ferme's fire are
other terms, while " Corbie's Aunt " is a term
employed in the North-East of Scotland.[1]

It is mentioned by Masoudi, by Pliny, in his
Natural History, by Horace and Seneca. In the
Middle Ages, when the patron saints of Christianity
took the place of the old sea-gods of Greece, this
electrical phenomenon was attributed to the Saint
St. Elmo who became the patron saint of sailors, and
the light was looked upon as an indication of the
guardian's presence, come to warn sailors of any
misfortune in store for them. The Spanish mariners
called it *cuerpo sante*.

The light was perceived by the crew of Columbus
on his second voyage. A sudden gust of wind had
come on during the night and the crew considered
themselves to be in great peril, but suddenly one of
the sailors saw the flame playing about the tops
of the mast and gliding along the rigging. He called
the attention of his comrades to it and the whole
crew rejoiced, convinced that St. Elmo, their protector, was near. This was indeed the body of St.
Elmo and they held it now for certain that no one
on board their vessel was in danger.

[1] See Mélusine, IV, col. 214.

This nautical superstition is also mentioned in the history of the voyage of Magellan. The crew welcomed the presence of the Saint during several great storms when he appeared at the topmast with his lighted candle and sometimes with two. The sailors were overjoyed, but the Saint disappeared with a great flash of lightning.

An interesting scene is described in a sea-novel.[1] On a night of storm and rain one of the sailors suddenly perceived blue flames playing in the rigging. The flames excited my curiosity.

" What is it ? " I asked one of the sailors.

" St. Elmo's light, Sir," he replied.

" Ah, the light of St. Elme ? It does not burn ? "

" Burn ? It is the friend of the sailors and their consolation."

" But how can you believe in such superstitions," I asked. " It is only an electrical effect."

" Electrical, as much as you like," he said, " but it is nevertheless true that this little flame which is resembling the flame of a glass of spirits set on fire is the soul of a poor mariner who had been drowned. When dirty weather is threatening, these poor sailors appear in the shape of the blue flame to warn their comrades."

" I am going to touch your soul of a dead sailor," I said. " I tried to do so, but the light seemed to evade my touch."

[1] *Le Négrier*, by Ed. Corbière.

" Shall I make it disappear ? " cried a Breton sailor.

" Yes," I replied.

He made the sign of the cross and the light suddenly vanished. Thus coincidence naturally strengthened the superstition of the sailors.[1]

A further description of this superstition so widely spread among sailors of all nations and of all ages, is given by an author of the nineteenth century.

" By seven in the evening a fine southerly gale brought us within six or seven leagues of the anchorage of Palma Bay. About this time the sea-breeze failing us astern, was shortly succeeded by light and baffling breezes off the land. No sooner had the setting sun withdrawn the golden beams from the top of the lofty hills, than a thick and impenetrable cloud, spread darkness on the hills below. The darkness was intense, rendered more sensible by the fire that gleamed upon the horizon to the South, and aggravated by the deep-toned thunder which rolled at intervals on the mountain, accompanied by the quick rapidity of that forked lightning, whose eccentric course and due effects set all description at defiance. By half-past nine the hands were sent aloft to furl topgallant sails and reef the topsails, in preparation for a threatening storm. Suddenly a cry of ' St. Elmo ' was heard

[1] Mélusine, II, col. 116.

SAILORS RETURNING FROM A SEA VOYAGE

from those aloft, and fore and aft the deck. The
awestruck mariners, bareheaded, on their knees,
uplifted their hands in voice and attitude of prayers
to St. Elmo. The lightning continued with un-
diminished intensity for ten minutes, when it disappeared, and the seamen, sure of their preservation,
finished the work they had left undone."[1]

A French author of the eighteenth century[2]
gives the following description of this superstition :

" Towards midnight our sailors perceived Helena
at the topmast. This light resembles somewhat the
flame of a candle of an ordinary size and is bluish
in colour. On these occasions the sailors first
recite hymns and litanies and when, as it often
happens, the light still remains, they salute it by a
whistling sound. When the light vanishes, they call
after it : ' Lucky journey,' and if it reappears again
the whistling begins. The sailors are firmly convinced that this light is St. Elmo, the protector of
mariners who comes to inform them that the
tempest is at an end."

They assert that on a certain vessel where the light
of St. Elmo had appeared, a sailor climbed up the
mast and there found a few drops of wax which
no doubt came from the wax-taper the Saint is
holding in his hand. The Sailors are so convinced
of their idea that when the chaplain on board

[1] See Jones, *Credulities*, p. 76.
[2] Père Chomé, *Lettres édifiantes et curieuses*, Lyons, 1819, Tome
5, p. 130.

wished to dissuade them of this superstition, they looked upon him as a heretic.[1]

In Cornwall the lights are called Jack Harry from the name of the first man who was fooled by them. The lights are generally observed before a gale.

Breton sailors believe that the St. Elmo's lights are souls in pain, usually blood-relations of those who perceive them ; they implore the latter to recite prayers and masses for their erring souls. Some sailors believe that they are old drowned sailors who are trying to get on board the ship where they had served and are asking to be remembered in the prayers of the crew. On the island of Batz the light of St. Elmo is supposed to be a malevolent spirit resembling a will-o'-the-wisp which appears on the shore to fascinate sailors.

When the light of St. Elmo illumines the head of a sailor working in the mastyard it is a sign that his hour of death is near. The same superstition is found among American sailors.[2] German sailors, on the contrary, believe that when the head of a seaman working in the mastyard is illumined by St. Elmo's light, there is no reason to be frightened, for the Saint is only helping him to complete his work speedily. French sailors say that if the light of St. Elmo is double it represents St. Elmo and

[1] See also Mélusine, IV, col. 381–2.
[2] See Dana, *Two Years before the Mast*, p. 340.

St. Nicolas, but if it is treble it is a sign that St. Barbe has joined the two saints and is a sure indication of fine weather. In Portugal, too, seamen consider the appearance of St. Elmo's light as an indication of fine weather. German, British, and American sailors are convinced that if the light of St. Elmo appears in the rigging it indicates fine weather.

Among the legends explaining the origin of the light of St. Elmo the following two are interesting :

Once upon a time there was a captain who met a shipwrecked man in the open sea, carried along by the current in a small canoe. He brought the stranger on board his vessel, took care of him and landed him at last at a certain place. Now this stranger was none other than Saint Elmo. When he found himself safe on the shore he asked the captain how much he owed him for the service he had rendered him.

" I require nothing," replied the captain, " for what I have done. I did it for the love of God and have acted as other sailors in my place would have acted. You told me that you were a Saint. Now saints can work miracles. Work a miracle to prove to me that you have spoken the truth."

" Since you refuse to accept money," replied the Saint, " I will express my gratitude in some other way. When a storm is near, I will send a light which will warn you and other sailors of its approach.

Whenever you perceive my light at the top of your mast, you will know that a storm is near."

Thereupon St. Elmo wished the captain a lot of prosperity and ascended to Heaven in the presence of the crew.

The captain was lucky in his sea-journeys, thanks to the light of St. Elmo which warned him of an approaching storm so that he was always able to seek shelter. Ever since the light of St. Elmo appears to sailors to warn them of an approaching storm.[1]

Another legend, explaining the origin of the light of St. Elmo, runs as follows :

Once upon a time there was a hermit named St. Elmo. He went about begging for alms and everybody gave him something. One day this Saint's brother died, leaving behind him seven sons in the direst misery and want. St. Elmo took his nephews with him, but now the charitable people who used to give him alms ceased to do so. St. Elmo prayed to God to help him, and his prayer was heard. He suddenly beheld a giant holding a lantern in his hand.

" I am St. Christopher," said the giant, " and I have been sent by God to help you by means of this lantern."

St. Elmo, greatly wondering at such a strange and miraculous assistance, prostrated himself before St. Christopher.

[1] Sébillot, l.c., p. 95 ; Mélusine, II.

" This lantern," said the latter, " will be lit on the sea on nights of stormy weather. It will render good service to and save from danger poor sailors and smugglers."

St. Elmo, acting upon the advice of St. Christopher, placed his lantern upon a rock in the sea. By its light sailors steered their course on dark and stormy nights and never forgot to express their gratitude to St. Elmo. Henceforth the Saint returned home with his knapsack full and he could thus bring up his nephews.[1]

[1] *Ibid.*

WINDS AND STORMS

Thus the wretched Shawondasee
Breathed into the air his sorrow ;
And the South-Wind over the prairie
Wandered warm with sighs of passion,

With the sighs of Shawondasee,
Till the air seemed full of snowflakes,
Full of thistle-down the prairie,
And the maid with hair like sunshine
Vanished from his sight for ever ;
Never more did Shawondasee
See the maid with yellow tresses !

Poor, deluded Shawondasee !
'Twas no woman that you gazed at,
'Twas no maiden that you sighed for,
'Twas the prairie dandelion
That through all the dreamy Summer
You had gazed at with such longing,
You had sighed for with such passion,
And had puffed away for ever,
Blown into the air with sighing.

Oh, deluded Shawondasee !
Thus the Four-Winds were divided ;
Thus the sons of Mudjekeewis
Had their stations in the heavens,
At the corners of the heavens ;
For himself the West-Wind only
Kept the mighty Mudjekeewis.

LONGFELLOW, *The Song of Hiawatha*,
The Four Winds.

CHAPTER III

WINDS AND STORMS

The spirits of the wind—Odin on his horse Sleipnir—Winds
looked upon as gods—Luther's opinion—The myth of the
Four Winds—The Song of Hiawatha—An evil spirit hidden
in the whirlwind—Gustr and Blaster—The rebel spirits—
Winds leading the life of seamen—Weather indications—The
sound of the waves—The song of the sea in Scotland—
Porpoises announce stormy weather—Omens from fishes—
Omens from birds—Seagulls—Magpies and pigeons—Tempests—Superstitions connected with—Mermaids indicating
a storm—Sea-urchins—Black human shapes—The souls of
drowned seamen—The Squire of Bottreux—The bells of Boscastle—Superstitions of Breton sailors—Tempests the direct
work of the gods—A Chinese superstition—Tempests due
to undesirable persons—Priests and Sisters of Mercy—The
story of the seaman Joseph—The Russian captain who neglected
to pay his debts—Windmakers—Witches possess the power
to raise storms—The belief of King James VI—Agnes Sampson—Mrs. Leckie—Wind knots—The sellers of winds—
The women of Winchelsea—The sorcerers of Lapland—Three
knots in a handkerchief—The Virgin and the Saints—St.
Nicolas, the ruler of the waves—Whistling for a favourable
wind—Scratching the mast with the nails—An old broom
thrown into the sea.

TERRIBLE and dangerous the winds have
always appeared to the mariner in general,
and to the seafarers of antiquity in particular. Here was reason enough for superstitious
fear and credulities. In his weary state of mind
and his strained nerves, the sailor saw the spirits
of the wind running through the air, roaring,
bellowing, and destroying, waging a fierce battle with

the clouds. During the dark gruesome night the men of the North heard one-eyed Odin rushing along upon his horse Sleipnir—the prototype of the wild huntsman—accompanied by the uproarious souls of heroes. The howling winds preceding the storm are the souls of women driven along by Odin. But the real gods of the sea are Ægir and Niord.

Everywhere the winds are something alive, animate, whether as Zephyr gently swelling the sails or as Boreas unto whom the Greeks offered sacrifices before the battle of Magnesium. He is the aquilo of the Romans and the typhoon, the terrible son of the netherworld, emerging from the depth with his hundred dragon heads, howling and roaring. He is still alive in the typhoon.

Winds have been looked upon by primitive nations and the early mariners as gods worshipped for their power. Later on they became demons or giants. This belief prevailed during the Middle Ages. Thus Luther believed that winds were nothing else but good or evil spirits, while St. Thomas wrote that rain and wind could be produced by demons.

" Among the native races of America," writes Tylor, " the myth of the Four Winds is developed with a range and vigour and beauty scarcely rivalled elsewhere in the mythology of the world. Many episodes belonging to this branch of Red Indian folklore have been collected in Schoolcraft's *Algin*

Researches, and thence rendered in Longfellow's masterpiece, ' The Song of Hiawatha.' The myth of the Four Winds runs as follows : The West Wind, Mudjekeewis, is Kabeyun, Father of the Winds ; Wabun is the East Wind, Shawondasee the South Wind, Kabibnokka the North Wind. Another mighty wind not belonging to this mystic quaternion is Manabozho, the North-West Wind, the unlawful child of Kabeyun. The fierce North Wind, Kabibnokka, in vain strives to force Shingebis, the lingering diver bird, from his warm and happy winter lodge ; and the lazy South Wind, Shawondasee, sighs for the maiden of the prairie with her sunny hair, till it turns to silvery white, and as he breathes upon her, the prairie dandelion has vanished."[1]

In many parts of Poland a belief still exists according to which an evil spirit is hidden in the whirlwind, while in Sicily superior beings are supposed to produce the wind. A powerful blast of wind is not a natural phenomenon, but the devil let loose. The Macingo is also a devil accompanied by evil spirits who takes the shape of a powerful blast.[2] A similar belief exists in Spain, and Victor Hugo evidently referred to such beliefs when he wrote : " Le diable était caché dans le vent qui soufflait."[3]

In the language of sailors winds and demons are

[1] See Tylor, *Primitive Culture*, Vol. I, p. 361.
[2] Pitre, p. 528.
[3] *Légende des Siècles*.

often connected. The Northern peoples believe
that the spirits of the air produce the wind and
are known as Gustr and Blaster. The Scandinavians represent the wind as a giant in the
shape of an eagle. And the winds issue from
underneath his wings whenever he spreads them
out for flight.[1]

There is a belief current in Brittany according to
which the winds are the inhabitants of the Ocean
who have been cursed on account of their revolt
against the sea. Their punishment consists in being
condemned to blow until the day of the Last Judgment.

Seamen's tales in ancient and modern times
attribute an important rôle to the winds, imagining
them as animate beings, incarnations of lower
divinities, of demons and spirits. They generally
dwell on the mountain-peaks or in caverns, the
abodes of the winds. Here they live under the
command of the North, their captain, awaiting his
orders to issue forth and blow over the ocean or
the earth. Sometimes their mother resides with
them.

Sailors imagine the winds as leading the life of
seamen on board a vessel. Some are working, while
others who have accomplished their day's task are
playing cards to beguile their leisure. They are
subject to many vicissitudes, and, like human beings,

[1] See *Revue Brit.*, 1871, III, p. 343.

can be wounded or hurt. Sometimes a strong
sailor can defeat the wind and compel it to give him
some talisman by means of which he is enabled
to obtain all that he desires.

Sailors and fishermen who have constantly before
their eyes the spectacle of sea and sky and who are
passing almost their whole existence upon the vast
expanse of the water, are naturally led to examine all
the phenomena they are witnessing. They are
drawing conclusions from various indications and
think that they can predict the weather. There
are old sailors whose knowledge of the atmospheric
phenomena is such that they are often able to predict the weather conditions quite correctly. By the
side, however, of such prognostics, based upon experience, there are others which are of a purely
superstitious character. Thus some sailors pretend
that the sea, which is a living being, feels beforehand
what the weather is likely to be and indicates this
by peculiar noises and sounds. This sound is
either gay or lugubrious and plaintive.

In Brittany, when the sea is singing on the shore
or at the foot of the cliffs, they say that it is braying
like an ass. Fishermen listen attentively to the sound
of the waves and pretend that they can predict the
weather a week hence. At St. Malo, when the sea
emits a ringing sound, it is supposed to predict the
approach of north-eastern winds.

Scottish fishermen say that if the song of the sea

is heard from the west, it is a sign of fine weather.[1]
English sailors call the plaintive sound coming from
the sea " the calling of the sea," and when it is
quite clear it is supposed to predict bad weather.
Fishermen on the Moray Firth call the sound of
the waves " the song of the sea," and pretend
that if this song comes from the east it is a sure
sign that an east or south-eastern wind will
soon begin to blow. If a long song comes from the
bar of Banff it is a sign that an eastern wind is
coming.[2]

Sailors also believe that the fish possess a sort of
instinct which enables them to feel the coming
weather. Thus in Brittany they say that three
days before dirty weather the fish quickly take
the bait, but on the day on which a change of the
weather is to take place they never come near
the lines. If the large fishes are swimming on the
surface of the water it is a sure sign of wind. French
sailors say that porpoises announce stormy weather,
while dolphins are never so happy and never caracol
so joyously as at the approach of stormy weather.
When dolphins are rolling in the sea it is a sure
sign of an approaching breeze.[3]

In France, in Scotland, and in Germany sailors
maintain that porpoises are always swimming towards the wind, going out to meet it. Bernardin

[1] *Folklore Journal*, 1885.
[2] Gregor, *Folklore of N.E. of Scotland*, p. 155.
[3] Gregor, *Folklore of Scotland*, p. 127.

de St. Pierre[1] already made mention of this belief. Old fishermen pretend that at the approach of a fierce wind the whale is agitated and is seen to jump up high, and the higher it jumps the fiercer will be the coming wind and storm.

Not only fishes but sea-animals, too, are supposed to feel the approaching wind and storm. Thus when conches cling to the rocks or when crabs seize stones or go down deeply into the sand it is a sure sign of rain and wind.

In Brittany and in many other maritime countries sailors and fishermen pretend that winds never blow fiercely without the birds announcing their approach. Magpies never chatter so much as before a coming wind; swallows approach the trees and keep on one side, while pigeons are pursuing each other, beating the air with their wings. Both in Scotland and in Poitou the belief exists that when sea-birds are flying inland in groups and are making a great noies it is a sign of an approaching hurricane.[2] When the seagulls assemble on land it is considered in Brittany as a sign of bad weather, while in England and Spain the gathering of gulls on the seashore predicts a hurricane. The stormy petrel or, as it was called, Mother Carey's chicken, cautions seamen of the approach of a tempest. In Picardy and in Finistère sailors call it the storm bird.

---

[1] *Voyage à l'île de France.*
[2] See Gregor, *Folklore of Scotland*, p. 134.

TEMPESTS

Many superstitions connected with tempests still prevail among sailors and fishermen. Thus sailors on the coast of Charente in France pretend that a tempest usually lasts three, six, or nine days. On the coast of the Finistère the belief is current that a tempest never abates until the impure bodies and corpses have been thrown on the shore. In other places there is a custom to light wax-tapers in the houses during a tempest, and the manner of their burning and the movements of the flame are so many indications of the fate in store for the sailors in the open sea. Norwegian sailors look upon the appearance of a mermaid as a sure sign predicting a storm.

To see a mermaid is a sure sign of a coming storm. " Sailors and fishermen," writes Thorpe, " are afraid when mermen and mermaids rise from the bosom of the tranquil deep. The mermen are of a dusky hue, with long beard and black hair. From the waist upwards they resemble a man, but downwards are like a fish. The mermaids are beautiful upwards, but downwards, like the mermen, have a fish's form. Their children are called marmachler. These are sometimes caught by fishermen, who take them home, that they may gain from them a knowledge of future events ; for both they, as well as the mermen and mermaids, can see into futurity. It is now rare to hear a mermaid speak or sing.

Mariners are not pleased at the sight of them, *as they forbode a storm.*"

It is dangerous to hurt them. A sailor once enticed a mermaid so near that she laid her hand on the gunwale of the vessel which he struck off. For this barbarity he was overtaken by a storm, in which he nearly perished. St. Olaf, on one of his piratical expeditions, fell in with a mermaid, who by her sweet song was wont to lull mariners to sleep, and then drag them down. If, in diving under water, they turn towards the ship, it betokens misfortune ; if they turn from the ship, it is a good sign.[1]

Sea-urchins thrusting themselves in the mud, or striving to cover their bodies with sand, forbode a storm ; when a tempest is near, cockles and most shell-fish are observed to have gravel sticking hard to their shells, as a providence of nature to stay or poise themselves, and to help to weigh them down if raised from the bottom by surges.[2]

Masoudi writes that before a tempest there are apparitions on board of ship. There used to be belief among Chinese sailors that every time when the sea is very rough and the waves are running high, black human shapes like little Abyssinians suddenly emerge from the water and come on deck. Whatever their number they remain harmless, but their

[1] Thorpe, l.c. II, pp. 27–28.
[2] Jones, l.c., p. 15.

appearance is a sure indication to the crew that a terrible storm is in store for them. In Cornwall fishermen never dare pass the night on the shore near a place where ships have been wrecked. The souls of the dead sailors are said to be haunting these places. This happens under certain circumstances, but particularly before a storm. Many a fisherman pretends that he had heard the voices of the dead sailors calling out their own names.[1]

The dead, according to some superstitious beliefs, are supposed to leave their wet graves in the water and to warn the living of the coming storm. The inhabitants of the island of Slin say that three days before a fierce storm a concert of lamentations is heard in the air. Often a piercing, heart-rending cry, as a sort of supreme appeal, is heard in the midst of the confused noise. On the coast of Scotland numerous spectres are said to issue forth from the sea just before a storm.

There is a belief in Wales according to which the sound of the bells of the Squire of Bottreux is heard to issue from the depth of the sea before an approaching storm. It is said that once upon a time the Squire of Bottreux wanted to make a present to the people of Boscastle of bells as large as those of Tintagel. He shipped the bells on a vessel and when the latter was already in sight of Boscastle the pilot wanted to sound the chimes of his country,

---

[1] See R. Hunt, l.c., p. 367.

as a thanksgiving for the happily accomplished
voyage. But the captain said that thanks were due
to the solidity of the vessel, and as for ringing the
bells there was plenty of time to praise the Lord
when they would have landed. Immediately a
fierce storm arose and ship and crew with the
exception of the pilot sank.[1]

There is a belief prevalent on the coast of Brittany
that the drowned choose the times of storm to
recall their memory to their parents and relatives.
At such moments there are as many phantoms
hovering on the shore as there are of the other dead
on the night of Toussaint or All Souls' Day.

In the neighbourhood of St. Malo people believe
that during a storm the souls of the sailors for whom
no mass had been read come to wake up their
parents.

In the neighbourhood of Tréguier the inhabitants
say that during a storm they can hear strange sounds
which are attributed to the sound of bells, bells
which are ringing in the depth of the sea. Such
are the bells of the city of Is, of St. Gildas and
others. When the sound of the bells is heard, it is
a sign that the tempest will last many days.

Tempests have often been personified. We find
this idea not only in the Greek and Roman mythologies, but also in that of the Scandinavians where
the tempest is assimilated to a bird.

[1] *Tour du monde*, XI, p. 389.

In ancient times tempests were supposed to be the direct work of the gods who presided over the destiny of the seas. Sometimes lesser divinities, in the absence of their superiors, could also unchain tempests. Superstitions which are to some extent reminiscent of these ideas still prevail, or at least have prevailed until quite recently, among civilized and uncivilized nations alike.

Tempests have been attributed not only to gods who sent them to punish men who have incurred their anger, but also to mischievous demons. The latter find pleasure in annoying mortals. Fortunately these demons are sometimes either asleep or otherwise busy, and sailors therefore consider it advisable not to disturb them. A superstition also exists among Norwegian fishermen to keep silent when passing the abodes of the demons.

One day Chinese pilots, noticing that the Dutch cook had lit a fire to prepare dinner, implored on their knees the ambassadors to have the fire extinguished. In the lake of Po-yang, they maintained, there dwelt an evil spirit in the shape of a dragon or a fish who abhorred the smell of roast or boiled meat, and if such a smell came to his nostrils he would produce a terrible tempest and all the vessels would sink.[1]

Tempests are also supposed to be due to the presence on board a ship of an undesirable person.

[1] See Laharpe, VI, p. 289.

The first example of such a superstition is found in
the story of Jonah. The Greeks and Romans shared
this superstition and it is mentioned by Cicero and
Plautus. Priests, too, are considered to be undesirable persons and the cause of tempests. This
superstition is still prevalent among many sailors.
In the Middle Ages a priest on board ship ran the
risk of being thrown into the sea when a tempest
broke out, but even now sailors still dislike the
presence of a black-robed priest on board. On
some French vessels it is a Sister of Mercy who is
considered to be the cause of a tempest.

Dutch sailors believe that a tempest is due to
the presence on board ship of someone who has
either neglected to pay his debts or who has a grievous
sin on his conscience. The following characteristic
incident is related in *France Maritime*.[1]

During a heavy tempest the seaman Joseph, who
had embarked on the American vessel *The President*,
approached the second lieutenant and thus addressed
him :

" I alone am the cause of the heavy tempest
which is now raging. I am firmly convinced that
vessels on which I embark have to experience
terrible tempests and to battle against high seas.
I attribute this punishment to the sinful life which
I have been leading for years. The Supreme
Judge will never be satisfied, and the tempest will

[1] I, p. 204.

never cease until I shall have thrown myself into the sea."

Thus spoke the Breton sailor and, suiting the action to his words, jumped overboard. The vessel landed at Charlestown, but during its return journey to New York a tempest once more arose. All the sailors now cried that the vessel would certainly sink if the box containing the belongings of Joseph was not thrown into the sea. A Scotsman immediately seized the box and hurled it into the sea, while reciting a prayer and imploring God to cause the tempest to stop, since the sacrifice had been made. He also begged the drowned sailor's pardon. Gradually the tempest abated, and the courage of the crew revived. A few days afterwards, however, the tempest broke out anew. The sailors, still clinging to their superstition, began to search the vessel for some object which had belonged to the unfortunate Joseph. One of the sailors at last came across an old boot of Joseph which he immediately hurled into the sea.

A similar story of a tempest which is supposed to have arisen on account of an evildoer on board a ship is told of a Russian captain. He went to sea without having previously paid his debts. A terrible tempest arose and he was in such sore straits that he saw no other way out than that of throwing the box containing the cash into the sea. The remedy proved efficacious, and the storm abated.

A strong belief in human agency and the power
of man to raise storms existed during the Middle
Ages and is not yet extinct in our own days.
Various practices were also adopted by superstitious
sailors to influence the winds and to ensure prosperous passages to seamen. The belief in the power
of certain beings to make winds and raise storms
can be traced back to the seafaring tales of antiquity.
Thus we read in the Odyssey that Æolus and Calypso
possessed the power to control the winds.

In the fifteenth century the belief in witchcraft
was strong and, as a matter of fact, is not yet
entirely gone.[1] Witches were supposed to have
the power to raise storms. Reginald Scott wrote in
his *Discoverie of Witchcraft* as follows :

" No one endued with common sense but will
deny that the elements are obedient to witches,
and at their commandment, or that they may at their
pleasure send hail, rain, tempest, thunder and lightning, when she being but an old doting woman
casteth a flint stone over her left shoulder toward
the west, or hurleth a little sea-sand up into the
element, or wetteth a broom sprig in water and
sprinkleth the same into the air, or diggeth a pit
into the earth, and putting water therein, stirreth
it about with her finger, or boileth hog's bristles,
or layeth sticks across upon a bank where never a
drop of water is, or buryeth sage until it be rotten ;

[1] See *Folklore*, 1894, XXXIV, pp. 183–184.

all which things are confessed by witches, and affirmed by writers to be the means that witches use to raise extraordinary tempests and rain."

The belief, however, was entertained by King James VI of Scotland, who declared, on his personal experience, in his *Demonology*, that witches can raise storms and tempests in the air, either on sea or land.

In the year 1590 King James brought his bride from Denmark to Scotland, naturally by the sea-route. During the voyage a terrible tempest arose in the North Sea and the cause was attributed to witchcraft. The culprits were soon discovered. A certain Dr. Fian and a reputed witch of the name of Agnes Sampson were tortured and confessed their guilt, explaining with all details how they did it. It was not indeed the first time that Agnes Sampson and her sister witches had enjoyed the innocent pastime of raising storms.

One evening two hundred witches and sorcerers, each in a sieve, went on a sea journey—and in mid-ocean met Satan himself rolling upon a huge wave, resembling a haystack in size and appearance. The ladies went on board a foreign vessel which was richly laden with wine. Here the witches, naturally invisible to the crew, feasted and revelled and made merry, and when they had had enough, Satan, their master, raised a terrible storm and vessel and crew and all on board, with the exception of the old witches, went down.

In the case of King James VI, Agnes Sampson,
under the influence of torture, confessed that when
His Majesty was in Denmark she had taken a cat and
christened it. She thereupon took several parts of
a dead man which she bound to each part of the cat.
In the night following she and her sister witches
conveyed the cat into the midst of the sea, the
ladies sailing in their riddles or crieves. The cat
was then left right before the town of Leith in
Scotland. Thereupon a terrible tempest arose at
sea and caused the loss of many ships. There was
many a vessel coming from the town of Brunt
Island to the town of Leith, which carried sundry
jewels and rich gifts which should have been presented to the new queen of Scotland, when His
Majesty came to Leith. The christened cat was
also the cause of the terrific storm which His
Majesty's ship experienced, having a contrary wind
to the rest of the ships then being in his company.
This was a very strange phenomenon indeed, the
truth of which was admitted by the King himself.

The belief in the power of witches to raise tempests was still very vivid during the eighteenth
century.

Other stories of witches who were able to control
the weather and to raise storms and tempests are
related by John Dunton.[1] A certain old lady
named Leckie resided at Minehead in Somersetshire

[1] See Jones, l.c., p. 68.

with one son and a daughter. Mrs. Leckie made
herself so agreeable that her friends greatly regretted
the fact that such an excellent lady would soon be
lost to her friends on account of her great age.
To this Mrs. Leckie used to give the following
rather strange reply :

" Although you appear to like me now, you will
but little care to see or speak to me after my death,
though I believe you may have this satisfaction."

Mrs. Leckie died, and after her funeral she was
repeatedly seen in her earthly likeness, at home and
abroad, by night and by day. The resemblance,
however, was in feature only, for the conduct of
the ghost was the opposite to anything respectable.
She used to appear at noonday upon the quay of
Minehead and cry aloud : " A boat, a boat ! " and
if any seamen were in sight and did not come, they
would be sure to be cast away, as indeed they would
have been had they obeyed the summons.

This mischievous woman also ruined her own
son. He had several ships trading between England
and Ireland, but no sooner did his ships make land
and come in sight of England than the ghost of
the old woman would appear in the same garb and
likeness as when she was alive, and standing at the
mainmast would blow with a whistle. Immediately,
no matter how calm the sea was, a dreadful storm
would arise, wreck and drown ship and goods.

Another tradition of a witch who caused tempests

to break out exists at Peel, in the Isle of Man. An
old witch with a basin of water is reported to have
said that the herring fleet would never return ; and,
indeed, every ship was lost. The witch was then
put in a barrel with spikes and rolled down the hill.[1]
Not only witches but certain animals may be the
cause of tempests. The fear of witches who were
as a rule availing themselves of black cats was
transferred to the animal itself. Swedish sailors
refuse to take a black cat on board, for " it carries
storm in its tail."

The absence of the wind or a contrary wind are
most disagreeable and unpleasant for sailors, and it
was natural in primitive times to have recourse to
supernatural means both to produce a wind or to
render it favourable to navigation. The result was
that certain men, magicians and sorcerers, pretended that they possessed the power to control the
winds and to command the powers of the air to
send favourable winds to their clients. The belief
in the power of certain persons able to produce
or to change a wind is a superstition which has not
yet died out among seafaring people.

Wind Knots is the title of one of the legends told
by Thorpe. At Siseby on the Slei there dwelt a
woman who was a sorceress and could change the
wind. The Sleswig herring fishers used frequently
to land there. Once, when they could not return to

[1] Jones, l.c., p. 69.

Sleswig, the wind being west, they requested the woman to change it. She agreed to do so for a dish of fish. She then gave them a cloth with three knots, telling them they might undo the first and the second, but not the third until they had reached land. The men spread their sails, although the wind was west; but no sooner had the oldest of the party undone the first knot than there came a beautiful fair wind from the east. On undoing the second knot they had storm, and arrived at the city with the utmost speed. They were now curious to know what would follow if they undid the third knot, but no sooner had they done so than a violent hurricane assailed them from the west, so that they were obliged to leap into the water, in order to draw their vessel on shore.[1]

This story finds a parallel in another related by Peter McIntosh, in his *History of Kintyre*.

Old John McTaggart was a trader between Kintyre and Ireland. Wishing to get a fair wind to waft his bark across to the Emerald Isle, he applied to an old woman who was said to be able to give this. He received from her two strings, on each being three knots. He undid the first knot and there blew a fine breeze. On opening the second, the breeze became a gale. On nearing the Irish shore he loosed the third and such a hurricane arose that some of the houses on shore were de-

[1] Thorpe, III, pp. 23–24.

stroyed. On coming back to Kintyre he was careful to loose only two knots on the remaining string.[1]

Just as wind and tempest could be the result of human agency, so sailors believed, and still believe, that human *actions* could induce favourable winds to blow. Various practices were adopted for this purpose. Thus the women of Winchelsea were in the habit of turning a fane held by St. Lennard, the patron of the place. They turned the fane to such a point of the compass as best fitted the return of the seamen who were near and dear to them, such as husband, or lover.

The women of Roscoff in Brittany are still in the habit of sweeping out, after mass, the chapel of La Sainte Union and of blowing the dust towards that side of the coast by which their lovers and husbands are expected to come to them. This practice, they believe, will procure a favourable wind for their husbands or lovers.

In Brittany it was believed that certain sorcerers and witches had learned from the devil the secret how to produce winds and to travel in a whirlwind. Sometimes their expeditions through the air are not voluntary. Some of the witches who had sold their souls to the devil but had disobeyed him are imprisoned by the Prince of Darkness in a whirlwind, and are condemned thus to travel from one end of the world to the other without ever finding rest. If, at

[1] See Jones, l.c., p. 71.

the moment of a passing whirlwind, one succeeds
in throwing an open knife, preferably one with a
crooked blade, into its midst, one is sure of thus
delivering a tormented soul.[1]

In the seventeenth century there still prevailed a
belief in the North of Sweden according to which
the sorcerers of Lapland were able to produce
favourable winds and calm weather. They were
said to be able to stop a ship in its course. What
they most particularly could do was to sell a favourable wind to their clients. They made three knots
in a handkerchief which they handed to the buyer
of a wind. By untying the first knot the possessor
of the handkerchief could produce a breeze, by
untying the second knot he could obtain a fiercer
wind, a gale, but when he untied the third knot a
hurricane would at once begin to blow. This
manner of selling winds in Lapland was said to have
been quite usual, and the smallest sorcerer had the
power of thus producing winds.[2] In Scotland, too,
we find such wind merchants.

" Raising the wind " is a phrase which once described one of the sorcerer's most dreaded arts,
practised especially by the Finland wizards, of
whose uncanny power over the weather sailors
have not to this day forgotten their old terror.[3]
The name of Finn still remains among seafaring men

[1] Mélusine, II, col. 206.
[2] See Regnard, *Voyage en Laponie.*
[3] E. Tylor, *Primitive Culture*, I, p. 84.

equivalent to that of sorcerer. Lapland witches, too, had a European celebrity as practitioners of the black art.[1]

Just as storms can be raised by certain supernatural powers and also by human agency, so they can also be caused to abate, thanks to the interference of the Virgin and the Saints, or through incantations, sacrifices, conjurations and oblations. Catholic sailors are convinced that the Virgin Mary possesses more power over the sea than all the Saints put together. She is invoked in the midst of storms, and devout sailors pretend that they can see her walking over the waves or appearing in the clouds. It often happens even now to see the entire crew of a vessel make a collective vow which they promise to keep faithfully if the Virgin will save them from a storm. Sometimes a devout sailor will make a vow which he considers to be the most difficult to accomplish. Thus a French sailor once made a vow to find in Brittany the ugliest and most dissolute maid and to marry her. On his return home he conscientiously searched for such a maid until he found and married her. The Saints, too, are believed to possess the power of causing the storm to cease. Sailors in Brittany believe that St. Beuzec and St. Houarden have only to lift their fingers to calm the fury of any storm.[2]

---

[1] *Ibid.*, I, p. 115.
[2] Mélusine, II, 207.

Greek sailors say that St. Nicolas is the ruler of the waves and that during a tempest he leaves the port and walks upon the waves, wearing boots made of marine herbs. With his invisible arm he leads to a safe haven the sailors who invoke his aid. In Spain, on the shores of the Atlantic Ocean and of the Mediterranean Sea, when a storm prevents the boats from going out to sea, the fishermen attach a cord to the statue of the local saint and throw it into the sea. The superstition that certain incantations and propitiatory ceremonies had the power to stop a storm has always existed among seafaring people. Among Northern nations it was a science which formed part of the education of the Vikings. The superstition existed among the Scandinavians and the Anglo-Saxons and is still to be met with in the North of Scotland. The superstition also existed among the Moslem nations.

Sometimes sailors addressed their prayers to the Saint in a rather disrespectful manner, as the following description will show : The sea was calm, but the wind was not favourable. The Portuguese sailors addressed a prayer to St. Anthony, but it remained without effect. Thereupon the seamen were on the point of binding the image with ropes to the mast, when the pilot interfered and begged them to desist. He promised in St. Anthony's name a fair wind. The Saint, however, remained deaf, and his statue was ultimately bound to the

FISHERMEN
by Troyon

mast with a rope so as to compel him to send a favourable wind. Still St. Anthony remained obstinate, whereupon insults were heaped upon his head. When the wind at last began to blow and a fine breeze arose, the statue was delivered and carried back to its niche with all tokens of respect.[1]

Favourable winds can also be obtained by various means without having recourse to sorcerers or dispensers of wind. This belief still persists among many sailors and fishermen. Thus the sailors of Brittany say that if the sea is calm one has only to whistle, and old fishermen pretend that it only very rarely happens that the wind disobeys the summons. Sometimes a prayer addressed to St. Clement, " who rules the waves and the wind," and added to the whistle will prove efficacious. Should the Saint prove somewhat slow in responding to the invitation, one has to swear, to insult him and to call him Pierrot, and he will obey. This superstition exists in other parts of the world. On the coast of Finistère a breeze is supposed to begin to blow either when one whistles in a certain manner or in consequence of a prayer addressed to St. Anthony.

Old French sailors believe that when there is no breeze it is due to the fact that St. Anthony, the patron of the wind, is either asleep or cross. In order to wake him up, sailors swear at him, and as

---

[1] Pietro della Valle, quoted by Sébillot, l.c., II, p. 230.

he has forbidden whistling at sea they whistle for all they are worth.

Fishermen in the Asturias whistle for the breeze they require. Sailors in Scotland whistle softly when they are in need of a breeze.

In the Baltic Sea it is considered to be efficacious to whistle in an engaging manner if one wishes for a breeze. As there is danger of the breeze becoming a gale, it is advisable to stop between each whistle and to address to the wind a few flattering words such as : " Come along, old chap, come along, old boy."[1]

In Brittany, when there is a breeze and someone begins to whistle on board ship, he is immediately told to stop, as there is danger of the breeze becoming a gale or even a hurricane. Old sailors never whistle when the weather is threatening to get dirty, for fear of increasing the force of the wind by their whistling. In Norway, too, sailors say that whistling at sea calls forth a storm.[2]

The superstition according to which a breeze comes when one whistles for it, exists also among the Annamites. They whistle, only very softly, for fear of producing a gale or a hurricane instead of a breeze.

The following legend explains the reason why a breeze obeys the sailors' whistle :

[1] See Mélusine, II, col. 186.
[2] Mélusine, II, col. 188.

Once upon a time a mighty lord went out to sea
in a fisherman's boat, but was surprised by a calm
sea. Instead of advancing, the craft was carried
back by the current. Both the lord and the fisherman were greatly annoyed. Thereupon the fisherman, just to amuse himself, began to whistle, and
immediately a breeze began to blow. It was
Norouas who had come, and he brought the vessel
to port. The fisherman thanked Norouas for his
timely help and in token of his gratitude offered him
a bottle of wine. Norouas drank the bottle at one
gulp, for he was very thirsty. The fisherman
offered him a second bottle which Norouas put
into his pocket for future use.

Thereupon the fisherman said to the lord : " Sir,
without Norouas you would not be here now. You
ought to give him something for his trouble."

The lord was reluctant, but finally took out a
gold piece and offered it to Norouas. The latter,
however, refused the gift.

" Keep your gold," he said, " I do not want it, as it
was not given voluntarily."

And ever since the winds always obey the summons of the sailors when the latter whistle for them,
but they never come at the invitation of the lords.[1]

In Pomerania old sailors do not even go to the
trouble of whistling. They are so well known to
the winds that they have only to appear at the helm

[1] See Sébillot, *Légendes*, Vol. II, p. 248.

and to say : " Now, come along, old chap," and in
a quarter of an hour the required breeze makes its
appearance. They call, however, the wind not too
loudly but in a flattering and confident tone, otherwise there is danger of its becoming a gale.[1]

In the Baltic Sea the superstition exists that
when the wind is favourable it is dangerous to mention the fact, as the breeze does not like it and might
feel inclined to cease. On the other hand, one should
not express any fear that the wind might turn.
What is considered to be most dangerous is to
calculate the time when one will reach port.[2]

In Scotland, to have a favourable breeze, it is
considered to be efficacious to scratch the mast
with the nails.[3] This superstition exists also in
Germany, and sailors on board Hamburg vessels
scratch the mast with their nails.[4]

It seems that a curious superstition existed among
sailors, according to which husbands of unfaithful
wives enjoyed the privilege of being able to summon
a breeze.

Pomeranian sailors believe that in order to have
a favourable breeze one has only to throw an old
broom into the fire, turning the handle in the
direction from which one wishes the breeze to blow.
Should the favourable breeze still refuse to come,

[1] See Mélusine, II, col. 186.
[2] Mélusine, II, col. 186.
[3] *Folklore Journal*, 1885.
[4] Mélusine, II, p. 188.

one should throw overboard an old broom without
a handle—holding it in the direction whence one
wishes the breeze to come. The breeze is sure to
come at once. This remedy should, however, be
employed only in cases of absolute necessity, as there
is no telling how strong the breeze might be and one
runs the risk of producing a gale or a hurricane. A
great deal of harm would thus be caused to other
vessels. Quarrels thus frequently arise between the
crews of vessels meeting in open sea when the
sailors on board of one of the ships throw a broom
in front of the other.

In Normandy the wives of fishermen whose
husbands have not returned from their fishing
expedition when they are expected to, on account
of unfavourable winds, burn a new broom so as to
produce a favourable breeze.[1]

It is also considered dangerous to sew or mend
on board ship when there is an unfavourable wind,
for one runs the risk of sewing it on and making it
last. On the other hand, when a favourable breeze
is blowing, it is good to sew and mend, as this
operation will make the breeze last.[2]

[1] Mélusine, II, p. 232.
[2] Mélusine, II, p. 186.

FOLK-TALES OF WINDS AND STORMS

CHAPTER IV

FOLK-TALES OF WINDS AND STORMS

Folk-tales and legends of winds and gales—The shipmaster from
Aarhuus and the Finlap—The mysterious bag—The silver
spoon—The winds stored up in a distant country—The captain
who went to fetch the wind—The South-western wind let loose
—The man in search of his wife and the mother of the winds—
North Wind and his rebellious crew—The strike of the seven
winds—The King of France and the war with Spain—The
wind as a demon—King Solomon and Adares—The fierce
wind—The leather flask—The demon in the leather flask—
The immense corner-stone—Ephippas and the demon from
the Red Sea—The story of the lad who went to the North
Wind—The wonderful cloth—" Cloth, spread yourself "—The
ram who could coin golden ducats—The handy stick—The
charitable woman and the wind—The three loaves of bread—
The wind snatches a small sack of flour—The three merchants
—The leaking vessel—The service rendered by the wind—
The cave of the winds—The two brothers—The sea-journey—
The earthly Paradise—The apple from the Tree of Life—
The sick princess—The Lord of Coucy.

THERE is a Danish folktale which runs as
follows :

One day a shipmaster from Aarhuus was
lying at Drontheim, where he formed an acquaintance with a Finlap who often came on board to
visit him. This Finlap, who could perform many
sorceries, offered, among other things, to teach the
shipmaster how to procure a wind. This, thought
the shipper, might be very convenient, and the next
day the Finlap brought a bag with him which he

97

placed outside the cabin saying that he needed only
to take that with him, and he could make any wind.
But the shipmaster on reflection would have no
concern with it, suspecting that it came from the
devil. The Finlap then asked him whether he
wished to know how his wife and children were.
When the skipper answered in the affirmative,
the Finlap immediately fell down on deck as if
dead. After some time he rose saying : " I have been
to Aarhuus. Thy wife was sitting and drinking
coffee ; the others were also in good health, though
one of the children had been ill. That thou mayest
believe my words, dost thou know this ? " at the
same time handing him a silver spoon.

" This," said the skipper, " thou hast taken from
my house in Aarhuus." And so saying, he took the
spoon and kept it.

After they had been lying some time at Drontheim, the Finlap one morning said :

" To-morrow we shall be under sail, and shall
both have a good wind, although you are going
southward and I northward. And I will further
tell you that you will not go to Christiania Fiord,
to purchase a lading, as you think, but will get a
better freight than you expect."

On the following morning both were under sail,
and the wind changed so that the Jutlander had a
fair wind for twelve hours, and afterwards the Fin
for twelve hours. When off the isles of Öster-Riis

the wind for the Jutlander was directly adverse, so
that after having beaten about for nights and days
he was at last obliged to seek port in the Oster-Riis
Islands. There a merchant offered him a freight
to the Issefiord which almost equalled the value of
a whole lading. When he arrived home to his wife,
he enquired :

" How are all here ? "

" Well," was the answer.

" Has anyone been ill ? "

" Yes, the young one."

" Have you lost anything ? "

" Yes, a silver spoon."

" There it is," said the skipper, laying it on the
table.[1]

There are many seamen's tales in which the winds
are not supposed to have always been blowing
over the sea. They are said to have been stored
up in a distant country, and until daring mariners
came to fetch them there navigation was practicable
only by means of oars and of the tide. A Breton
tale relates the origin of the wind as follows :

Once upon a time there was a daring captain
who was sent to a distant land to fetch the winds
and cause them to blow on the ocean. There were no
winds in those days and seamen were obliged to
make use only of oars, which was very tiresome for
them. The captain landed alone in the land of the

---

[1] Thorpe, l.c., II, p. 193.

winds and placing them in watertight bags brought them to his vessel. His sailors were ignorant of the nature of the goods stored up in the bags, and the captain had forbidden them to touch or meddle with them. One day, however, one of the crew, driven by curiosity, said to his comrades : " I want to know what these mysterious bags contain. I will open one, and as soon as I will have satisfied my curiosity close it quickly." Going down into the hold, he opened one of the bags, which happened to contain the South-Western Wind (Suronäs) which immediately escaped and began to blow so fiercely that the crew were swept overboard and the vessel was broken into a thousand pieces. The other bags, too, were burst open by the winds which they contained. They escaped, and spreading over the ocean have been blowing there since.[1]

This tale reminds us, of course, of the Odyssey, where Eolus is said to have imprisoned the winds in a leather bottle which he handed to Ulysses. One of the crew having opened it paid with his life for his curiosity.

Another tale relates of a hero who was in search of his wife. In his wanderings he reaches the house of the winds and meets the old mother at home.

" Do you know," he asks, " the whereabouts of my wife ? "

[1] Sébillot, *Contes des marins*, No. 23.

" No," replies the mother of the winds, " but my children, males and females, may know."

The old woman, however, hides the hero so that the winds, on their arrival home, may not eat him. Questioned by their mother, the winds reply that they do not know where the hero's wife was, but one of them, Sirocco, in the end consents to lead the hero to the place where he would find his wife.[1]

The captain of the winds is the North Wind and it sometimes happen that his subordinates revolt against this savage and monstrous leader, always anxious to destroy everything in his way. This revolt is imagined by superstitious sailors, to whose imagination such tales are due, something like the revolt of the crew against a hard and cruel captain. One of these tales relates of the revolt of the seven winds against Captain North.

One day North, captain of the winds, sent his crew to blow over distant lands. They were dissatisfied, for they had been working hard for some time and had asked their captain for a few days' rest which he sternly refused to grant them.

" If this dirty dog of a North," murmured the crew, " persists in commanding us to blow continually without respite, we will soon fall ill or grow weak in the chest from so much exertion. Let us revolt against him, let us strike."

" Yes, let us strike," cried the seven winds who

[1] Politis. *Météorologie*, p. 32.

constituted the crew. They all went to the North
Wind, and their spokesman, the South-Westerner,
thus addressed the latter :

"We are tired and exhausted and have no
strength left in our bodies to blow any more. We
must have some rest, and if you insist on our blowing
continually we shall soon waste away and die. I,
for my part, am wounded in the leg by an arrow
sent by a man whose garden I had damaged. We
are working hard, Captain, while you are staying at
home confortably."

Thus spoke the South-Westerner, and at a sign
from him all the seven winds hurled themselves
upon North Wind with the intention of killing
him.

Enraged at this speech the North Wind began
to blow fiercely, hurling all the other winds and either
throwing them upon the ground or lifting them up
in the air. Too weak and exhausted to resist the
fierce onslaught of their captain, they were compelled to beat a retreat. On the following day,
however, feeling a little rested, the rebels appeared
again and this time they proved the stronger. In
vain did the North Wind call for help, no one came.
The rebels were on the point of cutting the throat
of their captain, when suddenly the sound of trum-
pets and the clanging of arms were heard. It was
the King of France who was returning home with
his army from a war. The North Wind begged the

King to come to his aid and the sovereign hurried
to the assistance of the captain in distress. The
seven winds, however, began to blow with such
force that the soldiers of the King of France were
scattered on all sides. Fiercely did the seven winds
blow, uprooting trees and destroying everything
in their way. A moment came, however, when, their
fury spent, they were exhausted, and the King
quickly made use of this short respite. Calling his
soldiers, he commanded them to fire against the
rebels. This they did, and the seven winds, who had
never heard such a noise, were greatly frightened.
They ceased to blow and begged their captain,
the North Wind, for forgiveness, swearing obedience
and submission. Thus the revolt came to an end,
and the fierce North Wind was happy and content.
He now invited the King of France and his soldiers
to enter his castle where he made them welcome.

" Have you been victorious in the war ? " asked
the North Wind.

" The war," replied the King of France, " is not
yet over and to-morrow's battle will decide of our
fate."

" And against whom are you waging war ? "
again queried the North Wind.

" Against the Spaniards," replied the King of
France. " They have gained one battle but been
defeated in another. If, however, they carry off a
victory to-morrow we are lost.

"Fear nothing, sire," said the North Wind. "Pass to-morrow on your way to the battlefield and I and my seven sailors will accompany you and fight on your side."

On the following morning the King of France called for the North Wind and his seven sailors who were ready to accompany him. The King offered his newly-found allies horses and weapons, but the winds accepted only the horses, refusing the weapons which, they said, would only impede them in their fight. Mounting the steeds, the winds advanced in front of the army and thus faced the enemy. When the signal for battle was given, the eight winds began to blow so fiercely that the Spanish soldiers were lifted up high in the air, dancing and turning like so many flies.

"The devil," said the Spaniards, "is among the French."

The King of Spain, greatly frightened, begged for peace, and the winds ceased to blow. The Spanish soldiers now fell down upon the ground, but they were all dead. The King of France granted peace, but on condition that the throne of Spain should belong to him. To this request the enemy was compelled to acquiesce, and the son of the French King immediately became King of Spain.[1]

The personification of the winds is found in the

---

[1] Tale told by F. Marquer in 1882 ; see Sébillot, *Légendes de la Mer*, II, pp. 192-195.

polytheism not only of the lower, but also of the higher races, and even in Jewish folklore, the folklore of the race which is the originator of Monotheism par excellence, there are tales representing the wind as a personified power. We find this personification in Eolus and Odin, or Woden, and in the Polynesian Maui. He is the East Wind, or he holds all the winds with the exception of that of the West in his hands ; he imprisons the winds with great stones rolled to the mouths of their caves, save the West Wind which he cannot catch or imprison, so that it almost always blows.[1]

The chief of the Polynesian wind gods were Voromatautoru and Tairibu, brother and sister, whose dwelling was near the great rock, which was the foundation of the world. Tempests and hurricanes, and all destructive winds, were supposed to be confined with them. The latter were employed by the chiefs to punish such as had neglected the worship of the gods. In stormy weather the compassion of the wind-gods was sought by the tempest-driven mariner at sea, or by his friends on the shore. It was believed that liberal presents offered to the winds had the power to purchase a calm. When the inhabitants of one island feared an invasion from those of another, they immediately carried large offerings to the winds, and besought

[1] See Ellis, *Polynesian Researches*, Vol. I, p. 129 ; Grey, *Polynesian Mythology*.

them to destroy by gale and tempest the hostile fleet whenever it might be put to sea.[1]

This superstition of offering presents to the wind or the wind-god is found in Carinthia, Swabia, Tyrol, and the Upper Palatinate. A wooden bowl containing various meats is set up on a tree before the house, to propitiate the wind that it may do no harm. When a storm rages a spoonful of meal is flung in the face of the gale, and the wind is asked to subside, since he has had meal for his child.[2]

The wind as a demon is represented in the following legend of King Solomon.

The power of Solomon over the demons became so great that he could subdue even the fiercest among them. Thus one day, Adares, the King of the Arabians, sent a message to King Solomon, of whose wisdom and power over all the spirits of the air he had heard, begging him to deliver Arabia from a terrible demon, who, in the shape of a fierce wind, blew over the country from early dawn until the third hour.

" Its blast," wrote the King of Arabia, " is so terrible and so harsh that neither man nor beast can withstand it, but are slain."

The King of Arabia, therefore, begged the King of Israel to send a man and capture this terrible demon, promising, in return for this act of righteous-

---

[1] See Ellis, l.c., Vol. I, p. 329.
[2] See Wuttke, *Deutscher Volksaberglauben*, p. 86.

ness, that he and his people and all his land would
serve King Solomon, and that Arabia would live in
peace with him.

Thereupon King Solomon called one of his trusted
servants and ordered him to take a camel, and also
a leather flask, and to betake himself to Arabia
where the evil spirit, fierce and terrible, was blowing.
Solomon also gave his trusted servant his signet
ring and thus he spoke :

"When thou wilt reach Arabia and the place
where the evil spirit bloweth so fiercely, place the
signet ring in front of the mouth of the leather
flask, and hold both of them towards the great and
terrible blast of the spirit. When thou wilt see that
the flask is blown out then hastily tie up its mouth,
for the demon will be in it. Then thou wilt seal the
flask with the seal ring very securely, and placing
it upon thy camel bring it hither. On the way,
no doubt, the demon will offer thee gold, and silver,
and much treasure to let him go free. Take heed not
to be persuaded, but try to find out from the demon
and make him point out the places where there are
treasures and gold and silver. Now, fare thee well,
and bring the demon from Arabia hither without
fail."

Thus spake King Solomon, and his trusted servant
did as he had been bidden, and set off into Arabia
to the place where, fierce and terrible, the demon was
blowing and blasting.

And when he arrived into this region of Arabia he waited till dawn, when the fierce and evil spirit began his daily blast. Facing the demon's blast, the messenger from King Solomon placed the leather flask upon the ground and held the ring on the mouth of the flask, so that the demon blew through the finger ring into the flask and blew it out. And when the servant of King Solomon saw that the flask was blown out, he knew that the demon was in it, and he promptly drew tight the opening of the flask in the name of the Lord God. He then sealed the flask securely with the seal ring, even as his master had bidden him do, but he tarried three days in the country to make trial. And lo ! the fierce and terrible wind had ceased, for the demon now shut up in the leather flask no longer did blow against the city. And the Arabs marvelled greatly and praised the Lord God who had given such wisdom and power to King Solomon.

They then heaped gifts upon the servant of King Solomon, and sent him away with much honour. And when the messenger returned to Jerusalem he placed the leather flask containing the demon of Arabia in the Temple.

Now it came to pass that just at this moment King Solomon was in great distress. The Temple was being completed, but there was an immense corner-stone which had still to be placed on the pinnacle of the Temple, and this work neither workmen nor demons had as yet been able to accomplish. Work as they might, they were not strong enough to stir it and lift it up to put it in its allotted place. Now on the next morning, after the return of his messenger from Arabia, the King went into the Temple and sat in deep distress, thinking about the heavy stone which neither workmen nor demons had been able to stir from its place. And lo ! the flask containing the fierce demon from Arabia stood up, walked around seven steps, then fell down and did homage to King Solomon. The latter commanded the demon in the flask to stand up and tell him his name and employment. King Solomon then said to the demon :

" Who art thou and by what angel art thou frustrated ? " And the demon replied :

" I am the demon called Ephippas and I am able to remove mountains and to overthrow them."

" Canst thou raise this stone," asked King Solomon, " and lay it in its place ? "

" Verily," said the demon, " I can do this, and, with the help of the demon who presides over the Red Sea, I can bring up a pillar of air and support the gigantic stone."

Thereupon King Solomon commanded Ephippas to become flat, and the flask to appear as if depleted of air. He then placed it under the stone, and behold, the demon lifted up the stone on the top of the flask, and put it in its appointed place. And then the demon who presides over the Red Sea appeared and raised a column of air and the pillar remained in mid-air supporting the stone. King Solomon asked the spirit who had come up from the depth of the Red Sea to tell him who he was and what was his business. And the spirit replied :

" I, O King Solomon, am called Abezithibod, and I once sat in the first heaven, being the descendant of an archangel. Fierce and winged I was, but I plotted against every spirit in Heaven. It was I who hardened the heart of Pharaoh, when Moses appeared before him ; and also in the time of the Exodus of the Children of Israel, it was I who excited the heart of Pharaoh and caused him and all the Egyptians to pursue the Children of Israel through the waves of the Red Sea. And it came to pass that when the Children of Israel had passed through the waves of the Red Sea, the waters came over the hosts of the Egyptians and hid them, and I, too, remained in the Sea." Thus spake the demon Abezithibod ; and King Solomon wondered greatly, and praised the Lord.[1]

THE LAD WHO WENT TO THE NORTH WIND

Once upon a time there was a poor old widow who had one son, and as his mother was feeble he went into the safe to fetch some meal for cooking. When

[1] *Testament of Solomon ;* see F. F. Fleck, *Wissenschaftliche Reise,* II, p. 3 ; *Zeitschrift fuer Historische Theologie,* 1844 ; Conybeare in *Jewish Quarterly Review,* Vol. XI, pp. 1–45.

he got outside the safe and was going down the steps, the North Wind suddenly came along, puffing and blowing, caught up the meal and hurried away with it through the air. The lad went up into the safe for more, but once more the North Wind came and carried it off. When the North Wind repeated his action a third time, the lad got very angry, and thought that he would look up the North Wind and ask him to give up his meal.

So off he went. The way was long, but at last he came to the North Wind's house.

" Good day," said the lad ; " thank you for coming to see us yesterday."

" Good day," replied the North Wind, in a loud and gruff voice ; " thank you for coming to see me. What is it you want ? "

" Oh," answered the lad, " I have only come to ask you to be so good as to let me have back the meal you took from me yesterday, for we have nothing else in the house to live on."

" I have not got your meal," replied the North Wind, " but if you are in such need I will give you a cloth which will help you to get everything you require. You will only have to say : ' Cloth, spread yourself and serve up all kinds of good dishes ! ' "

The lad thanked the North Wind for his kindness and set off with the cloth. As he was a long way from home, he stayed the night in an inn. Here he laid the cloth on a table and bade it serve him up all kinds of good dishes for supper. The cloth obeyed, and the lad had a fine supper. Now the landlord who stood by set his heart on the cloth, and when the lad wa. asleep he took the cloth and put another in its stead, just like the one he had got from the North Wind.

When the lad woke up in the morning, he took the cloth and went off with it. When he got home to his mother he said : " I have been to see the North Wind who is quite a decent fellow. He gave me a cloth which possesses wonderful virtues."

" Let's see," said the mother. The lad laid the cloth on a table and bade it serve up, but of course it did not serve even a piece of dry bread.

The lad hurried back to the North Wind who as payment for the meal he had taken gave him a wonderful ram who could coin golden ducats. As this gift, too, was stolen from the lad at the same inn where he passed the night, he hurried back again to the wind who now gave him a stick.

" If you say," explained the wind, " ' Stick, stick, lay on,' it will lay on until you call : ' Stick, stick, stop.' "

The lad was well content and went off. He had guessed by this time where his cloth and ram were. So when the landlord, who easily saw that the stick must be worth something, was on the point of stealing it while the lad was pretending to be

fast asleep, the lad called out : " Stick, stick, lay
on ! "

The stick began to beat the landlord until he gave
up both the cloth and the ram, and the lad went home
with the gifts he had received from the kindly North
Wind.[1]

The following Jewish folk-tale represents the
wind as a personified individual.

THE CHARITABLE WOMAN AND THE WIND

In the days of King Solomon, peace be upon him,
there lived a charitable woman who was always
ready to do good.   Although not rich herself, she
constantly gave away of her possessions to others.
Every day she baked three loaves of bread, two of
which she distributed among the poor, keeping
the third loaf for herself.   One day a stranger
knocked at her door, and thus he spoke :

" I was sailing in a vessel with all my possessions
when a storm arose and broke my craft.   All my
companions and the pilot perished and I alone
escaped, thrown on the shore by the waves.   I am
tired and exhausted, as I have not tasted any food
for three days."

When the charitable woman heard these words,
she immediately fetched one of the loaves she had
baked and offered it to the hungry stranger.   There-

[1] Asbjornsen and Moe, *Norske Folkeeventyr ;* see Dasent,
Popular Tales from the Norse, 1859.

upon she sat down and prepared to consume the
second loaf herself, when another stranger appeared
on her threshold.

" My dear lady," he said, " I was kept a prisoner
by enemies, but managed to escape three days ago.
I have not tasted any food ever since, and I implore
thee to have pity on me and give me a piece of bread
so that I may appease my hunger and not die."

The woman immediately handed the stranger
the second loaf and praised the Lord, who had
afforded her the opportunity of bestowing charity
upon the needy and the hungry.

Thereupon she produced the third loaf and prepared to make a meal, when a third beggar suddenly
appeared and asked for bread.

" On the road," said he, " I was caught by robbers,
but I escaped into the forest. For three days I have
lived on roots and herbs, and I have forgotten the
taste of bread. Have pity on me and give me
some to appease the pangs of my hunger."

Unhesitatingly the charitable woman offered him
the third loaf, leaving none for herself.   Thereupon she said unto herself :

" I will see whether I can find some more flour
in the sack and bake another loaf for myself." The
sack, however, was quite empty, and the woman
went out into the fields to gather a few grains of
wheat. She collected a handful of grains, carried
them to the mill, and had them ground to flour.

Carrying her small sack upon her head, she was walking home when suddenly a gust of wind came from the sea and snatching the small sack, hurled it away into the distance. The woman's hopes were thus frustrated, and she remained without bread for the day. Bitterly did she cry, exclaiming in her despair:

" Lord of the Universe! What sin have I committed that I should thus be punished?"

She went to King Solomon to complain of her misfortune. On that day the High Council had been convened by the King of Israel, and the woman thus addressed the members of the Sanhedrin:

" Ye judges in Israel, tell me why hath the Lord punished me thus that I, who have given of my substance to the hungry, am compelled to suffer the pangs of hunger myself?"

Whilst she was thus speaking, three merchants who had landed from their boat entered the judgment hall.

" Our Lord and King," said the merchants, " take these seven thousand gold pieces and distribute them among the noble and deserving poor."

Said King Solomon: " What has happened to ye that ye are so willingly giving away in charity so much gold?"

Thereupon the merchants told their story: " We were sailing in our vessel, which was laden with costly merchandise, and were already approaching the shore, when we suddenly noticed that the boat had a leak. We looked round for something to stop the hole but found nothing suitable. The boat was about to sink, and we seemed to be doomed to drown with all our belongings. In our dire distress we prayed to the Lord, and thus we said :

" ' Lord of the Universe ! If we reach the shore safely then we will give away to the poor the tenth part of the costly merchandise which we are carrying in our vessel.'

" Thereupon we fell upon our faces and in silent prayer awaited a miracle or death. And so great was our distress that our senses were troubled, and we never noticed that our vessel had in the meantime safely reached the shore. Thereupon we calculated the value of our merchandise and found that the tenth part of it was exactly seven thousand gold pieces. This money, faithful to our vow, we have now brought to thee, and beg thee to distribute it among the poor."

Thereupon Solomon, the wise King of Israel, asked the merchants :

" Know ye the exact spot where your vessel did leak, and did ye notice how the hole was stopped ? " To which the merchants replied :

" This we know not, for in our joy and our anxiety to come here we never investigated the matter."

" Then go and examine your vessel," said the

King, who had already guessed the truth. The merchants went away and soon returned with a small sack of flour.

" This sack," they said, " had, unbeknown to us, stopped the hole in our vessel."

Turning to the pious and charitable woman, Solomon asked : " Dost thou recognize this sack of flour ? "

" I do," replied the woman ; " it is the very sack I was carrying on my head when the gust of wind snatched it away and hurled it into the distance."

Thereupon King Solomon said :

" The seven thousand gold pieces are thine ; it is for thy sake that the Lord wrought this miracle. The Lord never forsakes those who walk in His ways." Thus spoke King Solomon, and the members of the High Council and all present admired the wisdom of the King of Israel.

The cave of the winds is referred to in another Jewish folk-tale.

Once upon a time there lived two brothers in Coucy, one a great scholar, but very poor, whose name was Moses, and the other very rich, called Haim. One day the rich brother asked the poor to go with him on a ship as he wished to speak to him privately on some important matter. He had engaged his brother as his adviser and for his services promised to provide for his family. During their voyage a storm suddenly arose and carried the ship to a part of the sea which was frozen. They saw a number of other ships driven there and stuck. The two brothers put a plank between one ship and another and thus succeeded in crossing over into the other ships where they hoped to see human beings, but they found that the people were all dead and their names inscribed on the sides of the ship. While the rich brother was gathering up all the riches which he found in the ships, his poor brother made a list of the names written on the sides of the ship. The two brothers at last came to a very high wall. Cutting a hole in the wall with his knife to make a foothold, the poor brother succeeded in climbing up the wall until he reached the top. His rich brother followed him, but the jewels which he was carrying pulled him back. He called out to his brother, but the latter could not hear him, so high was the wall.

The rich brother then crawled back to his ship which was richly laden with food, while the poor brother wandered along until he found himself in a dense forest. Here he remained for thirty days, living on the fruit of the trees, until he came to a white plain and perceived a castle in the distance. Suddenly he beheld a young man clad in white coming out to meet him. He recognized one of his former pupils who had died some time ago—and who told him that the place he had come to was the Earthly Paradise.

The wanderer continued on his way until he came to a mountain in which was a cave covered by a curtain. He lifted the curtain and saw that it was the cave of the storm winds. They began to blow immediately and uprooted many of the trees in the forest. They also blew over the frozen part of the sea and drove the ship wherein was the rich brother out to sea again into running water. Haim, the rich brother, was thus saved and could return home where he also provided for his brother's wife and children.

In the meantime the dead pupil came out again to tell his master that he had asked the Elders for permission to allow him to enter the Earthly Paradise, but that they had refused him entrance because he had lifted the curtain and thus loosed the storm without permission. The young man now directed his master on the right road, telling him where he would find human habitation. He also gave him an apple from the Tree of Life.

As soon as the poor brother smelled the apple he felt quite invigorated. He knew at once that through this apple the dead could be brought to life again. On and on he now wandered until he came to a town where he found many Jews. They were all in great mourning, because the King's daughter who was lying dangerously ill had been given up by all the physicians. The Jews were very sorry for the daughter of the King, but a great calamity was threatening also themselves. The King had asked them to pray to their God to heal the princess, but should their prayers remain without effect, they would be driven out of the country and their belongings and possessions confiscated.

When the lucky possessor of the apple from the Tree of Life heard the news he immediately sent a message to the King, informing him that he could heal the princess. When the courtiers saw him they laughed at him, for he looked poor, and his garments were torn and tattered. The King, however, summoned him into his presence and commanded him to try his skill on the princess. Moses made the patient smell the apple from the Tree of Life and thus restored her to life. Great was the joy of the King when he saw that his beloved child had received a new lease of life, thanks to the skill of the stranger. Moses was offered money and a high position at Court, but he refused both the money and the position. When the King insisted on his naming his reward, he replied :

" I only want to be appointed Governor of my native town."

" That is very little," said the King, " for the service thou hast rendered me in restoring to life my beloved child."

Moses, however, insisted, and the King granted his request. He sent word to the town that a large palace should be built for the new Governor, and the work lasted a year. Now the King was anxious to learn from Moses the secret of his daughter's cure and invited the Jew to accompany him on a sea-journey where he hoped to be able to persuade his guest to reveal his secret to him. Moses at first hesitated, but at last gave the King the apple to smell, and the latter at once felt young and vigorous. Afraid, however, lest the King keep the apple and proclaim himself a god, Moses pretended to slip and thus dropped the apple into the sea.

The new Governor then went to his native town, where no one recognized him and he was lodged in the house of his brother, the richest man in town. As the latter had arranged to marry his niece, Moses' own daughter, to a man the father did not like, Moses made himself known and married her to another young man much superior in every way. The new Governor thereupon returned to his study, and having freed the town from all dues and taxes, he was henceforth known as the Lord of Coucy.[1]

[1] See Clouston, *Eastern Romances*, pp. 22 and 517; see also Gaster, *The Exempla of the Rabbis*, p. 140, No. 374.

ENCHANTED ISLANDS AND ROCKS

CHAPTER V

ENCHANTED ISLANDS AND ROCKS

Mysterious islands—The habitations of malevolent spirits—
Islands suddenly raised from the waters—The appearance of
green islands—The phenomenon of the mirage—Floating
islands—Mountains torn up by volcanic eruptions—The
roaring of wild beasts—The egg laid by a gigantic bird and
hatched by the sun—Islands created to give asylum to the
heroes in danger—The island of Ava—Islands fished from the
deep—Clods of earth thrown into the sea—Ireland a floating
island at the time of the Deluge—Gummer's Ore—The small
sand-bank of Helgoland—Islands guarded by dragons—
Monstrous giants as tall as a ship's mast—Islands inhabited by
graceful women—Jason and the island of Lemnos—The
islands of immortal women—Trees with suspended women—
Islands to which souls of the dead are carried—The rocks,
formidable assassins—Luonnotar, the mother of the waves—
Wainamoinen and his tinderbox—" An island shall be born "—
Rocks hurled by giants—The rock of the young girl—The
beautiful Gurri—The cursed stone—The fairy traversing the
sea of Jersey—The monk and the fisherman's wife—The
rocks on the coast of Illyria—The rock of Ortach—The Mermaid rock—The Nereids on the rocks.

ISLANDS surrounded on all sides by a tossing
and tumultuous sea have from time immemorial produced upon the minds of men
the impression of mystery. Numerous superstitions,
legends, and folktales cluster round their origin
and the beings who have their residence there.
Sailors still believe that some islands are the habitations of malevolent spirits who suddenly raise them
above the waters for the purpose of mocking and

annoying the navigators and mariners and upsetting
their calculations. There is a belief current among
seafaring people that at certain moments, when they
are suffering from hunger or are tortured by thirst,
green islands appear upon the surface of the ocean,
but can never be reached. This belief is no doubt
connected with the phenomenon of the mirage and
hallucination which is so frequent among the
shipwrecked. At such moments, while the ocean
all around is quite deserted, boats at full sail seem
to appear on the distant horizon.

On the Channel coast the belief in floating islands
is current, and sailors say that they are mountains
torn up from the bottom of the sea by volcanic
eruptions. Some sailors pretend that they have beheld such islands with their own eyes. They flee
before the vessels which can never reach them.
The islands are conducted by a demon in command
of the souls of the drowned who have deserved to
go to hell and are therefore condemned to remain
upon the mysterious islands until the Day of Judgment. The roaring of wild beasts can distinctly
be heard on some of these islands, and to encounter
them is considered by sailors as a bad omen.[1]

These beliefs and superstitions current among
seafaring people are the vestiges of the past and
are to be met with in the mythologies of various
nations.

[1] See Sébillot, *Légendes*, Vol. I, p. 349.

In a dim and distant past, say the inhabitants of
Hawai, when the ocean covered the entire surface
of the globe, an enormous gigantic bird laid an egg
which, hatched by the sun, produced the island
of Hawai. According to the Japanese, islands
were born from the union of Isanaghi and Isanami.[1]
The Polynesians relate that islands were hurled
down from heaven by the will of the gods. In
former times there were five moons in the firmament which cast a malevolent spell on those who
gazed upon them and who were suddenly affected
by a strange madness. The God Taarva conjured
these moons and hurled them into the sea where they
constituted five distinct islands.[2]

The Tahitians relate that once upon a time there
was a moon on the firmament more brilliant than
the present one. The gods, in divine sport, broke
it to pieces and hurled them into the sea. According
to many traditions, which can be traced to classic
antiquity, the islands were created by the gods for
the purpose of giving asylum either to gods who were
being pursued or to heroes in danger. Thus the
island of Delos, for a long time submerged under
the water, suddenly appeared upon the foam-
crested waves so as to give asylum to Latona.

The gods, relate the Japanese, hurled the island
of Ava into the ocean in order to help Hirougo in

---

[1] Metchnikoff, l.c., p. 266.
[2] See *Le Mariage de Loti*, p. 136.

his distress, when he was being carried away by the current in his light bamboo canoe.[1]

The islands, in the traditions clustering round the Pacific Ocean, are said to be fished out from the deep by the gods. Thus Isanaghi, the god of the Japanese, was one day searching the sea with his rod to see whether any submerged world existed at the bottom, and he thus created the island of Onokoro.

According to a legend current both in Greece, in the Scandinavian countries and in Oceania, islands were formed by clods of earth thrown into the sea by the heroes and semi-gods. Jason commanded Euphemus to throw into the sea the clod which Triton had given unto him on the soil of Libya, and from it arose the island of Calliste. The *Edda* of Snorri relates that Gylf, King of Sweden, granted unto a young stranger as much land as could be ploughed by four oxen in one day. She harnessed four oxen which she had begotten with a giant, and the ploughshare entered so deeply into the soil that a part of the soil was torn up. The oxen dragged it into the sea and thus the island of Seeland was formed.

Numerous stories and legends cluster round floating islands which early mariners pretended existed in the ocean. Pliny mentions several such islands, and for a long time the belief existed that

[1] Metchnikoff, l.c., p. 265.

Ireland was a floating island at the time of the Deluge. The belief in floating islands existed during the Middle Ages and even in modern times. These legends relating to floating islands are no doubt due to the existence of huge ice-blocks swimming in the Polar Sea. Sailors pretend that the floating islands are the habitations of malevolent sea-demons who thus endeavour to mislead mariners. One of these islands was that of Gummer's Ore which appears among the reefs near Stockholm. Baron Grippenheim relates that he had in vain looked for this island when one day he suddenly perceived three points of land above the surface of the sea.

"This is no doubt Gummer's Ore?" he asked his pilot.

"I do not know," replied the latter, "but you may be sure that what we now see predicts either a heavy storm or an abundance of fish."

Many Norwegian traditions relate to floating islands. Far away in the open sea, in the straits of Helgoland, there is a small sand-bank called Sand-flossen; it is an excellent place for fishing, but is difficult to be discovered, because it is floating from one place to another. This sand-bank was not always situated at the bottom of the sea. In times of yore it was an island in the possession of a rich peasant of Helgoland who had built there a hut to shelter himself in the summer. Fishermen and mariners pretended that they had often heard sounds of laughter and of music and all sorts of noises coming from the sand-bank, which from time to time emerged from the sea like a charming island. That is why they avoided the spot.

On the Channel coast the belief in floating islands still prevails. Sailors say that they are mountains torn up from the bottom of the sea by the eruption of vulcanoes. Mariners also maintain that there are islands guarded by dragons to prevent a landing. Often a loud whistling is heard, and by this sound mariners know that they are near one of these islands. Islands lying at some distance from the ordinary route of ships and offering certain difficulties of landing naturally struck the imagination of mariners. Such islands were considered to be the residences of peculiar and extraordinary beings, of giants and amazons, of fairies and semi-goddesses.

A Tahitian told the navigator Cook of an island inhabited by monstrous giants as tall as a ship's mast. They were usually good-natured, but when their ire was roused they could seize a man and throw him into the sea as if he were a tiny pebble. Their strength was such that they could take upon their backs a big ship. The works of antiquity, inspired no doubt by the tales told by ancient sailors and mariners, speak of islands inhabited by women who offered hospitality to mariners and navigators, and surrounding them with the delights of a maritime Capua, made them forget the dangers of the sea and the aim and purpose of their voyage. The easy virtue of the women on the islands of the Pacific, who had nothing to refuse to the sailors, and even went so far as to get rid of their husbands, have no doubt given rise to many such tales.

The companions of Jason were retained for several days at the island of Lemnos by the women living there. The Danish hero, Olger Danske, was retained by a fairy upon an enchanted island just as Ulysses was retained by Calypso. Certain islands in the ocean are called by the Arab geographers " the islands of immortal women." There is a belief current at Fidji of an island inhabited by such women.

By the side of enchanted islands inhabited by graceful and attractive women there are supposed to be other islands peopled by monstrous and terrible beings. Arab navigators speak of strange islands inhabited by terrible beings. The forests covering the surface of the island of Wak are said to contain trees upon the branches of which, instead of fruit, are suspended, by their hair, the truncated bodies of women without arms or legs. According to a Scandinavian tradition the island of Hornum is haunted by the phantoms of thieves, murderers and shipwrecked mariners.

In Brittany there is still current a belief in islands to which the souls of the dead are carried in boats on summer nights. When the sea is calm, one can hear the sound made by the oars as they cut the water, while white shadows are seen hovering over the black vessels. In Terre-Neuve there is an island called the island of the Dead and which is supposed to be the refuge of the souls of all the drowned people.

THE ROCKS

At a certain stage of civilization man is inclined to ascribe to objects which excite at once his awe, fear and admiration, supernatural causes. On account of their strange forms, their enormity and the danger they present for navigation, mariners believe that rocks had not been created at the same time as the earth and the sea. They are not even the result of the action of the waves or of some other physical phenomenon. The rocks were a special creation of gods and genii who had placed them where they are for a special purpose. Sailors and seafaring folk, constant witnesses of the fury of the sea discharging its roaring waves upon the rocks, have attributed to the latter either benevolent or malevolent passions. A sailor of Normandy will often say : "The rock of Jean Beaufils has forgiven the vessel, but the Moulière will not spare it,"[1] and Victor Hugo speaks of the shoal of Hanois as one of the most " formidable assassins of the sea."[2]

Various origins have been ascribed to the rocks

[1] See Alph. Karr, *La Famille Alain*, p. 110.
[2] V. Hugo, *Les Travailleurs de la Mer*.

in the mythologies of nations. In the *Kalevala* we read that Luonnotar, the mother of the waves, advanced into the open sea where she created the rocks and gave birth to the reefs so as to bring death to mariners.[1] Other rocks had been brought into being by heroes or gods for their defence. Thus Wainamoinen, menaced by the vessel of Pohjola, drew from his tinderbox a small piece of German tinder and a tiny pebble of flint, and throwing it over his left shoulder into the sea exclaimed : " A reef shall be born, and a hidden island shall arise, and may the vessel of Pohjola be broken against these rocks." And indeed from the German tinder and the flint a reef and an island emerged from beneath the waves and the hostile craft was hurled against them and broken.[2] Pausanias relates that Eacus had purposely dotted the neighbourhood of the island of Egina with rocks and reefs hidden beneath the waves, in order to defend the island against pirates and attacks of the enemy.[3] Neptune is said to have scattered islands and reefs in the Ægean Sea during his fight with the giants. Even to-day the natives of Hawai point out certain rocks which Pele, the goddess of the volcanoes, had hurled against the pirogue of Kahavari when that chief was fleeing from her wrath.

A number of rocks in Brittany are supposed to

---

[1] See Jones, l.c., p. 52.
[2] *Kalevala*, runo 43.
[3] Pausanias, *Journey to Corinth*, Chap. 29.

owe their origin to a giant who took them off from his boots, while others are the result of his digestions, and others again served him as projectiles against the enemy or the birds whom he wished to hit. There is a Norwegian legend according to which the rocks and reefs round the promontory of Kunnan were hurled by the giants during their fight.

In the Odyssey we read that the sirens, after the passage of Ulysses, were changed into rocks, or because Orpheus had surpassed them in song. Migne[1] relates that there is a tradition among mariners on the Baltic Sea that the rock known as the Moenslnit, or the rock of the young girl, is in reality a young and beautiful fairy who rules over the island and the waters. The white seen from a distance is her dress falling in folds. Gurri was the daughter of a giant, who dwelt on the isle of Kunnan off Helgoland. Being very beautiful, she had many suitors who fought for the possession of the fair giantess, and round about Kunnan is to be seen a cluster of rocks formed of the stones they hurled at each other. All were, however, forced to cede to the giant Anfind, who married the beautiful Gurri, and lived happily with her, until her father was slain, when the whole family was driven from Kunnan[2] upon the crests of the waves. She is the protector and patroness of mariners and especially of fishermen.

---

[1] In his *Dictionary of Superstitions*, col. 692.
[2] Thorpe, II, p. 8.

During the night one hears the sound of harmonious voices issuing from the waves bathing the rock. They are the voices ot other fairies who are coming to visit and pay homage to their queen.

There is a slanting stone, called the cursed, on a road at Tahiti of which the following tale is told : Taroa the creator had condemned this stone to roll eternally at the will of the waves without ever coming to rest. The stone thus rolled on for centuries until one day it perceived Tahiti. Tii, the god of night, seeing that the stone was anxious to have a rest, advised it to get on shore and to roll itself into the earth. Taroa could not see what was happening during the night and would not recognize the stone. One morning, however, the stone was surprised by the light of day and Taroa struck it. It has remained cursed and all those who repose in its shadow never awaken.[1]

Rocks are also said to emerge from the depth of the sea in order to help heroes in danger. One day a fairy was traversing the sea of Jersey when feeling somewhat exhausted she was anxious for a rest. Feeling a small pebble in her shoe, she took it off and shook it. The pebble fell into the sea and assumed such large proportions that the fairy could sit down upon it and have a rest. This is the rock of Verdelet near Pleneuf in the Côtês-du-Nord. According to a Provençal legend a monk

---

[1] Sébillot, *Croyances*, I, p. 320.

who was one day insulted by the wife of a fisherman hurled a curse against the pair. He threw a handful of sand into the sea and accompanied his action by a few mysterious words, and lo ! a reef suddenly emerged at the entrance of the bay against which the barque of the fisherman was smashed.

The Arab mediæval geographers believed that two African islands were suddenly changed into rocks by an angry god on account of the depredations of two pirate brothers who were dwelling there. Sailors also believe that other rocks, on the contrary, originally very dangerous, were made harmless by the gods. Such was the case of two rocks on the coast of Illyria. Seafaring people and mariners even at present believe that many rocks in the midst of the ocean are inhabited by malevolent spirits of the sea, by gods and genii. Sailors approach such rocks with awe and fear, or endeavour to propitiate the evil spirits residing there by various offerings and oblations. For a long time it was believed that the rock of Ortach, between Aurigny and les Casquets, was inhabited by St. Maclou, and many an old sailor pretended that he had actually seen the Saint sitting upon the rock and reading a book. Gradually the belief gave way to another. It was not the Saint but the devil who dwelt upon the rock, a devil named Jochmus who had for a long time given himself out as a Saint.[1]

[1] V. Hugo, *Les Travailleurs de la Mer*, I, Chap. II.

There is a rock on the Cornish coast, known as the Mermaid Rock, which is supposed to be haunted by a mermaid just before a shipwreck. In Eastern Prussia, at Nidden, a mermaid is said to be standing on a rock and calling the mariners, but long before the latter have reached the spot they are drowned. On the other hand, the Drowning Stol on the coast of Norway is supposed to be inhabited by the queen of the seas who is combing her hair and is bringing luck to fishermen. Greek sailors are still clinging to the old belief that the sea is inhabited by numerous tutelary and malevolent spirits, and some of them pretend that during the night they can perceive, on the rocks, the green tresses of the Nereids, who are alluring the mariners.[1]

Early mariners also believed in the existence of magnetic mountains. Mention is found not only in the *Travels of Sir John Mandeville*, but also in other works. In a twelfth-century poem of Henry of Waldeck, Duke Ernest and his companions sail into the Klebermeer where they see a rock called Magnes, and they are dragged in below among the wrecked ships whose masts stand like a forest.[2] This story reminds us of one in the *Arabian Nights*.[3]

[1] Thorpe, Appendix, I, p. 215 ; Jones, l.c., p. 61 ; Thorpe, II, p 56.
[2] Tylor, *Primitive Culture*, I, p. 374 ; Ludlow, l.c., p. 221.
[3] Lane, Vol. I, pp. 161, 217.

THE WORLD BENEATH THE WAVES

Forests at the bottom of the sea, the branches and leaves,
Sea-lettuce, vast lichens, strange flowers and seeds, the thick tangle,
  openings and pink turf ;
Different colours, pale grey and green purple, white and gold, the play
  of light through the water ;
Dumb swimmers there among the rocks, coral, gluten, grass, rushes
  and the elements of the swimmers ;
Sluggish existence grazing there suspended, or slowly crawling close
  to the bottom ;
The sperm-whale at the surface, blowing air and spray, or disporting
  with his flukes ;
The leaden-eyed shark, the walrus, the turtle, the hairy sea-leopard,
  and the sting-ray ;
Passions there, wars, pursuits, sight in those ocean-depths, breathing,
  that thick-breathing air, as so many do.

WALT WHITMAN.

CHAPTER VI

THE WORLD BENEATH THE WAVES

The world beneath the waves—Greek and Scandinavian mythologies—The Tsar Morskoi—Davy Jones—The beautiful country under the waves—The island of Fincara—Dermat o' Dyna visits Tir-fa-toun—The wizard-champion—The Knight of the Fountain and the Knight of Valour—The voyage of Maildun—The wonders of the deep—Submerged cities and sunken lands—The lost Lyonesse—The city of Is—King Grallon and his daughter—The cities built by men of a bygone age—The city of Berbido—Rouge-Gorge—The Isle of Man—The poets who have sung of the sea—Virgil and Kipling—Churches and bishops at the bottom of the sea—The fisherman who entered a church beneath the waves—Men who can live beneath the waves—King Souran—The Dutch seaman who asked for a pipe of smoke.

THE sea, on account of its depth, has always appeared to the mind of man as something mysterious. The belief has always prevailed that the depths of the sea were the abode of a particular world and inhabited by various beings either graceful or monstrous, terrible or benevolent. These beings dwelt in aquatic, transparent palaces richly ornamented with precious stones and wonderful plants. In Greek mythology Poseidon inhabits the depth of the sea and his magnificent palace is in the Ægean Sea. According to Hesiod the vigorous Triton dwells in a magnificent palace, and the Nereids have their dwellings

141

either in caverns or at the bottom of the sea. The Scandinavians believed that Oegir and Ran and his wife dwelt in the sea. Here, on the soft sand, Ran prepared his azure cushions for the ship-wrecked. The Tsar Morskoi, or the King of the Sea in Russian mythology, dwells at the bottom of the sea. The Eskimos believe that the Atalit are malevolent spirits dwelling at the bottom of the sea and are seizing the drowned. In the mythology of Greenland we read that the grand-mother or the daughter of the Tangarsuk dwells in the depth of the sea. A vase full of the oil of whales is standing above her lamp and various sea-birds are swimming therein. Sea-dogs are standing guard at the gates of her residence, biting all those who try to enter it.[1]

In the *Kalevala* we read that from time to time the queen of the waves emerges from the depth of the sea to the sweet song of Wainomoinen. The virgins of Wellamo, the maidens of the waves, are dwelling under the waves.[2]

According to the *Mahabharata*, the Daityas, or demons, after the death of their chief Vatra who was killed by the gods, took refuge at the bottom of the sea.[3]

English sailors believe that Davy Jones, the devil of the sea, dwells at the bottom of the ocean.

[1] Hans Egede, *A description of Greenland*, p. 182.
[2] *Kalevala*, XLI and V.
[3] See Mélusine, II, p. 365.

Numerous allusions to a beautiful country under the waves are found in Gallic tales. It is an enchanted land, sunk at some remote time, and still held under spell. It is called in some romantic writings, *Tir-fa-toun*, i.e. the land beneath the wave ; the heroes, on one occasion or another, find their way to it and meet with strange adventures. Remnants of this superstition are the island of Fincara, and the beautiful country seen beneath the waves by the hero Maildun. Sometimes it is known as *O'Brasil*, the dim land which appears over the water every seven years, " on the verge of the azure sea," and which would be freed from the spell and remain permanently over the water if anyone could succeed in throwing fire on it.

The tradition of a country under the waves is very old, for it is mentioned already by Plato in the legend of *Atlantis*, overwhelmed and sunk under the Atlantic Ocean at some remote time. The tradition also exists in the East.

> " I know where the Isles of Perfume are,
> Many a fathom down in the sea,
> To the south of sun-bright Araby."

In the Gaelic tale entitled : *The Fate of the Children of Turenn*, Brian and his brothers went out in search of the island of Fincara, sailing forth on the green billowy sea. They learned from an old man, who had heard of the island of Fincara in the days of his youth, that it lay not on the surface, but down

deep in the waters, for it was sunk beneath the
waves by a spell in times long past. Brian thereupon put on his water-dress, with his helmet of
transparent crystal on his head, and telling his
brothers to await his return, leaped over the side
of the ship, and sank at once out of sight. For a
whole fortnight he walked about in the green sea,
in search of the island of Fincara ; and at last he
found it. There were many houses on the island,
but one was larger and grander than the rest. Brian
entered it, and in a large room he saw a number of
beautiful ladies employed at all sorts of embroidery
and needlework. He took the long, bright cooking-
spit lying on the table which, on account of his
valour and comeliness which the beautiful ladies
greatly admired, he was allowed to carry off.[1]

In another tale, entitled : *The Pursuit of the Gilla
Dacker and his horse*, the hero, Dermat O'Dyna,
visits *Tir-fa-toun*. He met a wizard-champion
near a well with whom he fought, and who on
every occasion went down the well and disappeared
as if the well had swallowed him up. The selfsame
thing happened on three days, and on the fourth
day Dermat made up his mind to find out the secret.
When the wizard-champion was about to jump
down into the well, he closed on him and threw his
arms round him. The wizard-champion struggled
to free himself, moving all the time nearer and nearer

[1] See P. W. Joyce, *Old Celtic Romances*, 1879, pp. 87–89.

to the brink. Dermat held on, till at last both fell
into the well.

Down they went, clinging to each other, Dermat
and the wizard-champion. Dermat tried to look
round, but nothing could be seen save darkness and
dim shadows. At last there was a glimmer of light,
and the bright day burst suddenly upon them,
and presently they came to the solid ground, gently
and without the least shock. Here Dermat saw a
lovely country with many green-sided hills and
fair valleys between, woods of red yew trees, and
plains laughing all over with flowers of every hue.
He saw also a city of great tall houses with glittering
roofs, and a crystal palace, larger and grander than
the rest. He saw a number of armed knights
standing on the level green in front of the palace
who paid respect to the wizard-champion.

Dermat subsequently learned from the Knight of
Valour, who took him to his own palace, that this
country was *Tir-fa-toun,* and the wizard-champion
was king of the land and known as the Knight of
the Fountain. The Knight of Valour was his
brother on whose patrimony the king had seized.
Dermat entered into friendship with the Knight
of Valour and helped him to recover his inheritance.[1]

In the famous voyage of Maildun we are told
that the hero came to a lovely country beneath the
waves. Sailing on a sea which seemed like a clear,

[1] Joyce, l.c., pp. 248–259.

thin cloud, the hero, on looking down, saw beneath
the water a beautiful country with many mansions
surrounded by groves and woods. In one place
was a single tree, and standing on its branches
was an animal fierce and terrible to look upon.
Round about the tree was a great herd of oxen
grazing, and a man stood near to guard them,
armed with shield and spear and sword. When
he looked up and saw the animal on the tree, he
turned anon and fled with the utmost speed. Then
the monster stretched forth his neck, and, bending
his head downward, plunged his fangs into the
back of the largest ox of the whole herd, lifted him
off the ground into the tree, and swallowed him
down in the twinkling of an eye ; whereupon the
whole herd took to flight. With great difficulty
Maildun and his people got across the sea safely.[1]

In classic times a spell of terror was woven round
the Atlantic, but when it gradually began to lift
numerous islands swam into sight. But men were
still unacquainted with the various phenomena and
meteorological laws and, as in a glass, they saw
darkly many things not only upon the waves, but
beneath them. Things which appeared strange
to the early mariners were seen by the ancients in
the roaring waters. Sometimes in foggy weather
islands showed themselves, but once the mist was
lifted no trace of them remained. Gazing into the

[1] Joyce, l.c., pp. 147–148.

depth of the ocean in warm latitudes mariners saw
tall aquatic plants swaying slightly in the breeze,
and walls of coral gave the appearance of palaces.
The sea repeated in its mirror the sky and the
shore and the land beyond. These wonders gave
rise to beliefs and superstitions. There were groves
and gardens and habitations under the sea where
beings more beautiful than mortals lived and
roved in the dim peace of meadows situated beneath
the foam and tumult of the reefs.

There were submerged cities and sunken lands.
Sailors say that they often hear the sound of church
bells—peals that come from the ocean's depth and
float solemnly to the surface from towers beneath.
Fishermen pretend that when the sunshine falls
upon calm seas they can quite distinctly discern
the towers and the peaked roofs of houses. Numerous legends are clustering round these sunken
lands and cities of the deep. Such is the tale of the
lost Lyonesse, a great promontory of Cornwall, of
which the Scilly Islands are a remnant. Another
legend is the Breton tale of the city of Is, and the
peasants in Brittany point out the blocks visible
at low tide in the Bay of Donarnenez, which they
say are the foundations of the city. The story
runs as follows : The city of Is was built on a wide
plain below the level of the sea and a strong wall
with sluice-gates protected it against the encroaching
floods. Here dwelt Grallon, a blameless king, and

his daughter, Princess Dahut, a cruel, vicious and lustful maid. In her high tower Dahut entertained numerous lovers, drowning those she grew tired of. One day she stole the silver key hanging on a chain round her father's neck, opened the sluice-gates and let the sea in. Grallon, awakened by the tumult of the inrushing waters, mounted a horse and fled, accompanied by his daughter. The floods moved after him and a voice from above bade him sacrifice his daughter, the she-demon riding with him. The princess fell into the sea, and King Grallon reached Quimper where he rebuilt his residence. The city of Is was lost beneath the waves of the Atlantic, but Breton fishermen pretend that they can hear the chime of bells whenever wind and tide move shoreward together.

Beliefs in sunken towns are still current among sailors and people living on the coast. More than one Breton sailor will not hesitate to say that he had scanned the waves and discovered under the water long lines of walls, of castles, of gables, and spires of old churches. The narrators will pretend that on clear days in summer, when the sea is calm like a mirror, they have seen what they have seen. During the big tides they have even noticed, but for one moment only, suddenly emerging from the waves, tops of houses, and winding stairs. Everything under the waves is big and of vast dimensions, for the houses of the sunken towns had been built by men of a bygone age who were big and did everything on a large scale. Fishermen will assert that they can often hear the sound of bells, and they have other proofs of the existence beneath the waves of a busy life in the sunken towns. A sunken town is not necessarily a dead town. More than one town will one day emerge from the depth of the sea and once more occupy its place in the sun. On the coast of Morbihan they speak of a city under the waves called Berbido, and to describe a robust and strong lad they employ the expression : As strong as a fellow from Berbido. In the Finistère the story of the sunken town of Is is still vivid in the memory of the people.[1]

The notion of land under the waves is very widely spread and is common to many nations. We find it among the Aryans and the Semites, in Celtic lore, as well as in the *Arabian Nights* and in the Talmud. There is a story entitled *Rouge-Gorge*[2] where a maiden befriends a redbreast. By his aid and advice she gets magic sabots and a stick and is enabled to walk over the sea to certain islands. Here she knocks with her stick at a rock and out comes the sea-cow which is a cow in every respect, but magical and better than other cows. The maiden repeats three times the name of Saint Ronan d'Hybernie and strokes the beast with a

[1] See Melusine, II, col. 321–322.
[2] See *Foyer Breton*, 1858.

magic herle, whereupon the cow which had been sold
and had returned, is transformed into the sea-horse.
The horse is sold and returns and is transformed
by the same means into the sea-calf. It is a sheep,
with a red wool which is also sold, but jumps into
the sea, escapes to the Seven Isles, and vanishes
into the rock.

In another story a man goes into a boat like a
swan, and when he is on board the swan awakes
and dives to the bottom of a pool in the middle of
a sea-island, and there he finds a magnificent dwelling
and a fairy who treats him well for a time, but turns
him into a frog at last.[1]

In his *Popular Tales of the West Highlands*,
Campbell quotes from a curious pamphlet on the
History of the Isle of Man. The following tale
relating to mermen and a world beneath the sea
is interesting.

At Port Tron people were quite familiar with
mermen, and one moonlight night on the shore
caught a merwoman in a net. She would not
speak until she was allowed to escape to her own
people. She had a tail like a fish. Thereupon a
company was formed for diving " in glass machines
cased with thick, tough leather," and a man was let
down near the Isle of Man to seek for treasure.
The diver passed through the region of fishes,
and got into a pure element, clear as the air. He

---

[1] See Campbell, *Popular Tales*, Vol. III, p. 410 note.

saw the ground glittering with all sorts of magnifi-
cence, streets and squares of mother-of-pearl. He
hauled his diving-bell into a house, and almost
within reach of treasures, but there was no more
line and he was hauled back empty-handed. " The
main idea of the story," rightly observes Campbell,
" is that there is a world under the waves, and the
Manx sailors then declared that they commonly
heard at sea the bleating of sheep, the barking of
dogs, the howling of wolves, and the distinct cries of
every beast the land affords, and they now believe in
the water-horse and the water-bull and the seaman."[1]

Many poets, from Virgil to Kipling, have sung of
the sea. They have described the wide expanse
of the vast ocean, of wind, and storm, of the beauty
and grandeur of wind-swept ocean or of sea and sky.
Little, however, has been written on the wonders
and the beauty, the life and the grim tragedies in
the submarine world. There is a wonderful world
in the deep, there are secret gardens and blooming
sea-flowers unseen by human eyes ; coral beds of
poppy tints and myriads of living things dashing in
and out of coral castles. There are forests and
groves where sea-shells and pearls are tinted with
orient hues. No wonder that the superstitious
minds of early mariners have peopled the space
beneath the waves and the ocean's depth with a
wonderful world.

[1] Campbell, *ibid.*

There is a belief in the Scandinavian countries that churches and bishops exist at the bottom of the sea. The former often appear on the surface of the waters. Sailors say that the drowned men dwell in these churches until the Day of Judgment, and find there a rest as absolute as in the cemeteries on land.

One day a fisherman is said to have seen in the sea a house resembling a church and which seemed so solid as if it were supported by a rock. A big flight of stairs led up to its door. The fisherman, attaching a long cord to the highest step, entered the church where semi-obscurity and solemn tranquillity reigned. There were many persons who had been shipwrecked and some of them were clad in their fishermen's clothes which they had worn at the moment of their death. Afraid of meeting some of his comrades, the fisherman hastened to leave the building. It was high time, too, for already the church was beginning to sink, and the step to which he had attached his cord was already beneath the surface of the waters. He cut the cord, and he just had time to get on board his boat when the church disappeared under the waves.[1]

From time to time mortal men are supposed to have gone down to the bottom of the sea where they beheld a wonderful country and a new world.

[1] O. Nicolaissen, *Sagen on Eventyr fra, Nordland,* p. 30; see Sébillot, *Légendes,* Vol. I, pp. 199–200.

The belief that men can live beneath the waves is a widespread one and has existed since antiquity. Alexander the Great is said to have descended to the bottom of the sea in a glass case and to have seen vast treasures and wonders in the deep.

According to a legend of the Indian Archipel King Souran was curious to see the wonders of the deep. He had a glass case made which he could open and shut at will. The King was shut up in the case which was lowered to the bottom of the ocean. Here he saw treasures innumerable, and finally reached a land whose inhabitants were greatly surprised to learn that other countries existed elsewhere.

Souran married the daughter of the King of the submarine country, but as he was yearning to return to earth he craved the King's permission to do so and the latter gave him a horse named Paro-el-Bahri which carried Souran above the waves. The King alighted on the shore, and the horse returned to the bottom of the sea.

Another legend, showing how deeply rooted was the belief of the sailors that men could live beneath the waves, runs as follows :

In the beginning of the eighteenth century a sailor once jumped on board the merchant vessel *The Swallow*, commanded by Captain Baker, and asked the sailors, in Dutch, for a pipe to smoke. The man was covered with scales, and his hands

resembled the fins of a fish. On being asked who
he was, he replied that he was a Dutchman, that
he had gone out to sea at the age of eight years
and his ship having been wrecked he had lived
ever since in the sea.[1]

[1] De Maillé, *Telliamed*, 6th day.

THE DENIZENS OF THE DEEP

But at night I would wonder away, away
I would fling on each side my low-flowing locks,
And lightly vault from the throne and play
With the mermen in and out of the rocks ;
We would run to and fro, and hide and seek,
On the broad sea-wolds in the Crimson shells,
Whose silvery spikes are nighest the sea.
But if any came near I would call, and shriek
And adown the steep like a wave I would leap
From the diamond ledges that jut from the dells ;
For I would not be kiss'd by all who would list,
Of the bold merry mermen under the sea ;
They would sue me, and woo me, and flatter me,
In the purple twilights under the sea ;
But the King of them all would carry me,
Woo me, and win me, and marry me,
In the branching jaspers under the sea ;
Then all the dry pied things that be
In the hueless mosses under the sea
Would curl round my silver feet silently,
All looking up for the love of me.
And if I should carol aloud, from aloft
All things that are forked, and horned, and soft
Would lean out from the hollow sphere of the sea,
All looking down for the love of me.

A. TENNYSON, The Mermaid.

CHAPTER VII

THE DENIZENS OF THE DEEP

(MERMEN, MERMAIDS, KELPIES AND WATERSPRITES)

Land-animals and sea-animals—The story of the fox and the weasel
—Men and women in the sea—Belief in mermaids—A superstition among the North-American Indians—The fish-man who
tells of marvellous things—Mermaid anxious to acquire a soul
—The love of mermaids for music—The Ottawa chief and the
mermaid—The Adirondack youth—Beliefs in mermaids in
the Middle Ages—The Margyzr—Pontoppidan's views of
mermen and mermaids—The sailor and the mermaid—Dr.
Hamilton's account of a mermaid—Scottish fishermen not
afraid of mermaids—Pontoppidan's *Natural History of Norway*
—Description of mermen—The Marmaele—The superstition
of the peasants—The mermaid Isbrandt—The two Danish
senators—The " Nibelungenlied "—The hero Hagen and the
Mermaids—Mermaids anxious to decoy mortals—" The
mermaid," a poem by Leyden—A curious custom in the Isle of
Man—The annihilation of the wrens—Kelpies—The fisherman of the Dieppe and the watersprites.

THE belief that every creature on land has
its counterpart in the sea is still very
common among fishermen in Scotland.
Many fish are named after land-animals, as : the
sea-dog, the sea-soo, the sea-cat. When such come
upon the lines, this opinion is often given vent to.
Not only have land-animals their counterparts in
the sea, but also the vegetable kingdom on land,
according to some, has its counterpart in the sea.

Zoophytes go to the general name of sea-floors (flowers).[1]

The following folk-tale, in the *Alphabetum Siracidis*, illustrates this general superstitious belief :

THE STORY OF THE FOX AND THE WEASEL

And it came to pass that when the angel of death had closed and sealed the gates of the town which he had built for the bird Milham, the Lord of the Universe thus spake unto him :

" Throw into the sea a pair, male and female, from every species of the creatures I have created, and over all the others shalt thou have power." The angel of death obeyed and did as he had been commanded by the Lord of the Universe. He began to throw into the sea a pair from every species the Lord had created. When the fox—who was very wily—saw what was happening, he approached the angel of death and began to cry bitterly.

" Well, and why art thou crying so bitterly," asked the angel of death.

" I am weeping over my poor brother," replied the fox, " my brother whom thou hast just thrown into the sea."

" Where is thy brother ? " enquired the angel of death.

The fox approached and came up to the water's edge, so that his image was reflected by the water,

[1] Gregor, *Folklore Journal*, 1885, p. 183.

and pointing to his own image he said : " Here he is." When the angel of death saw the image of the fox in the water, he thought that he had already thrown one of the species into the sea. He therefore said : " As I have already thrown into the water one of thy species, thou canst go." And the fox ran away and was saved. On his way he met his friend the weasel, to whom he related what had happened and how he had cheated the angel of death and had escaped. The weasel greatly admired the cunning of the fox and did likewise. He, too, cheated the angel of death and was not thrown into the water.

Now it came to pass that after a time Leviathan, the king over all the creatures that live in the sea, gathered all his subjects round him, but he saw neither fox nor weasel among them. Greatly astonished, he asked the fishes why the fox and the weasel were absent and had not appeared in his presence. Then the fishes told Leviathan what had happened, how the fox and the weasel—who were both cunning and wily—had cheated the angel of death and been saved from the water. And Leviathan was very jealous of the fox and envied him his cleverness and intelligence and cunning. He therefore sent out the large fishes and commanded them to go and fetch the fox and to use cunning so as to entice him into the water and bring him before Leviathan. The large fishes did the bidding of

their King Leviathan, who is set over all the fishes in
the sea.   They swam to the shore and perceived the
fox who was walking up and down along the seashore.   When the fox beheld the large fishes who had
swum up he wondered greatly.

" Who are you ? " asked the fishes.

" I am the fox," he replied.

Then the fishes, who tried to be cunning, said :
" Hail, King !   Great honours await thee, for whose
sake we have come up to the surface of the waters
and swum up to the shore."

" How so ? " asked the fox.   And the fishes
replied :

" Our great King, Leviathan, who is the ruler of all
the creatures in the deep seas, is sick unto death.
Feeling his end near, he has decreed that none
but thou shouldst succeed him on his throne which
will soon be vacant.   He has heard of thee and how
clever and cunning thou art.   And he has dispatched
us, the large fishes, to find and bring thee before him
that he might crown thee king and leave his kingdom
to thee, for thou art cleverer than all the beasts of
the earth and all the fishes in the sea."

Thus spoke the fishes, and the fox was greatly
flattered and pleased to hear such tidings.

" But how can I go into the water," he said,
" without being drowned ? "

" Do not trouble about this," said the large fishes.
" We will carry thee upon our backs, as befits a

MERMAID

king. Right across the waves and over the vast
sea we will carry thee, until we bring thee before
our King Leviathan. And when thou wilt have
reached the abode of Leviathan thou wilt become
king over all of us, and thou wilt live happily for
ever. For thy nourishment will be brought to thee
daily, as it befits a king, and no longer wilt thou
fear the wild beasts who are mightier and stronger
than thyself."

And the fox listened to their voice and believed
their words. He mounted upon the back of one of
the large fishes who promised to carry him over the
surface of the waters to the abode of Leviathan.
But when the foam-crested waves began to beat
mightily against him, the fox suddenly felt afraid;
his heart fell and his ambition left him.

" Woe is unto me ! " he wailed. " What have I
done ? The fishes have deceived me and made a
fool of me. I, who have deceived and misled other
beasts, am now in their power, and who will save
me ? " And the fox thought deeply of means how
to escape. Thereupon he addressed the fishes and
said unto them :

" Tell me the truth, what is your purpose and what
do you intend to do to me ? " And the fishes said :
" We will tell thee the real truth. Our King
Leviathan, he who is the ruler over all the fishes
in the deep seas, has heard of thee and how cunning
thou art and he has said : ' I will cut open his

body and swallow his heart, and be as wise and cunning as the fox.' "

Then the fox said unto the fishes : " Why did you not tell me the truth at once ? I would then have taken my heart with me and offered it as a gift to the king. He would have honoured and loved me. But now evil will befall you, for your king will be angry, when he hears that you have brought me without my heart."

And the fishes marvelled greatly and said : " Is it really so that thy heart is not within thee and that thou hast come out leaving it behind ? "

" Verily, it is so," replied the fox, " for such is the custom among us foxes. We leave our hearts behind us in a safe place, and we walk about without any heart. When once we need it, we go home and fetch it, but if we do not require it our hearts remain at home in a safe place." Thus spoke the fox. And when the fishes heard this, they were greatly troubled and perplexed, and did not know what to do. But the fox said unto them :

" My abode is on the shore of the sea, just where you met me. If you will take me back to the water's edge, I will run up and quickly fetch my heart where it is hidden. I will then return with you to King Leviathan and offer him my heart as a gift. He will be greatly pleased, and honour you and me. But if you refuse and bring me to him without my heart, he will be mightily angry with you and will

swallow you up, for you have failed to carry out his
commands. As for myself, I am not afraid, for I
will tell him the truth. 'O Lord Leviathan!' I
will say, ' these fishes thou didst send out did not
tell me anything of thy desire. And when at last
they did tell me the reason of their errand, I urged
them to return and let me fetch my heart, but they
refused, and so I cannot offer thee my heart which I
would fain do.' "

When the fishes heard these cunning words of
the fox, they said to one another : " Verily, he has
spoken well." They returned to the seashore and
brought the fox to the dry land. The fox immediately jumped upon the shore, threw himself upon
the sand and began to dance for joy.

" Hurry up," urged the fishes, " and fetch the
heart where it is hidden, that we may return to King
Leviathan."

But the fox laughed merrily and said : " Verily,
you are fools. Do not you know that if my heart
had not been with me I could not have gone with you
upon the water and faced the foam-crested waves ?
Is there a creature upon earth that could walk
about without a heart ? "

And the fishes spoke : " Then thou hast deceived
us." But the fox only laughed and said : " If I
have been clever enough to cheat the angel of death,
how much easier was it for me to cheat you, stupid
fishes." And so the fishes returned to King

Levaithan empty-handed and were greatly ashamed.
When Leviathan heard their story he said :

" Verily, the fox is very cunning, but you are
very stupid and deserve punishment." He therefore ate them all. And ever since there are counterparts in the water of every species of beasts upon
earth, even the counterparts of man and of woman,
but there are none of either the fox or the weasel !¹

The belief that because there are men and women
on land, there must also be men and women in the
sea, gave rise to the superstitions about mermen
and mermaids, nymphs, sirens, kelpies and nixies.

The belief in mermen and mermaids, to which
some sailors still cling, is very old. We find the
conception in Babylonian, Semitic, and classic
mythologies. Oannes and Dagon, the tritons,
and the sirens, are represented as half-fish, half-
human. The belief in mermen and mermaids is
prevalent among the North-American Indians who
pretend that a fish-man had led them from Asia to
America. Jones, in his *Traditions of the North-
American Indians*, gives the following account of
this belief :

Once upon a time, the Indians relate, their
ancestors suddenly beheld a strange creature greatly
resembling a man riding upon the waves. He had
green hair upon his head and a beard of the same
colour upon his face which was shaped like that of

¹ *Alphabetum Siracidis.*

a porpoise. The Indians were terrified, and their terror increased when they noticed that from his breast down the man was actually a fish, or rather two fishes, for each of his legs ended in a fish tail. For hours this fish-man used to sit upon the waves, relating to the wondering Indians of the marvellous things which he saw in the water. He used to close his stories with the words : " Come with me, ye folk, and I will show ye many wonders." For many years the Indians refused to listen to the fish-man, but one day, when they felt the pangs of hunger, they yielded and ventured upon the water. Following the fish-man they ultimately reached the American coast.[1]

The belief that some mermaids are anxious to acquire an immortal soul and are yearning for the union with men, has given rise to the famous romances of *Undine* and *Melusine*.

Often, however, the case is the reverse, that is that the mermaid is captured and only reluctantly remains with her captor. When the latter is generous enough to give them their liberty they are grateful and show their gratitude in a practical manner. Thus one day a knight captured a mermaid and moved by her pleading, let her go. In token of his gratitude the mermaid saved the knight's life when his ship foundered.

The love of mermaids for music and song seems

[1] See Jones, pp. 47–58.

to be great. One day a mermaid had promised a fisherman wealth and power if he only came to live with her for three years. The fisherman consented, but his desolate mother who was desperate at the thought of her son leaving her, went to the seashore and here played and sang so long to the mermaid until the latter was moved. Rising upon the crests of the waves she returned her son to the sorrowing mother.

The belief that mermaids are anxious to acquire a soul is expressed in the following tale of the dwellers in the Canadian forests.

Sitting by the waterside, an Ottawa chief one day beheld a beautiful woman rising out of the flood. She was of exquisite beauty, with blue eyes, white teeth and floating locks. From her waist downwards she ended in a fish tail.

" Great warrior," she pleaded, " permit me to live on earth. I have no soul and I wish to acquire one, but this can only be done by my union with a mortal."

The warrior consented to grant the request of the mermaid and took her to his house where she lived as his daughter. Some years afterwards an Adirondack youth fell in love with the fish-lady and married her. She thus obtained a soul which she was yearning for. The tribe of the Adirondacks, however, was not pleased with this *més-alliance*, and the mysterious beauty was driven back

to her watery element. The water-spirits, enraged
at the offence thus offered to one of their tribe,
took their revenge and stirred up war between the
Ottawas and the Adirondacks which led to the
extermination of the latter. Only one man was
rescued and he was carried off by the mermaid to
the watery depth.[1]

The belief in mermaids is met with in the Middle
Ages, and we find it mentioned in the Icelandic
Doomsday Book at Landnama that a merman, or
marmennill, had been caught off the island of
Grimsey. In 1305 and in 1329 these beings appeared
off the coast. In another Iceland work called
Speculum Regali a description is given of a mermaid.

One day a monster was seen near Greenland
which people call the Margyzr. The creature
appeared like a woman down to her waist, with breast
and bosom like a woman, long hands and soft hair,
in short a woman in all respects. The hands, however, seemed to be rather long and the fingers
were not parted, but united by a web like that on
the feet of water-birds. From the waist downwards the monster resembled a fish with tail, fins
and scales. This creature is believed to show itself
at certain times, especially before storms. It
dives quite frequently and rises again to the
surface with fishes in its hands. When the sailors
see it playing with the fishes, or throwing them

[1] See Baring-Gould, *Curious Myths*, pp. 503-504.

towards the ship, they know that several of the crew are doomed to death. If, however, the creature flings the fish away from the vessel, then the sailors take it as a good omen and know that they will not suffer any loss during the coming heavy storm.[1]

The appearance of a merman is also recorded by the famous Pontoppidan in his *Natural History of Norway*.

Near Landscrona, about a mile from the coast of Denmark, three sailors perceived something resembling a dead body floating in the water and rowed towards it. At a distance of seven or eight fathoms from the floating object they noticed that it had not moved, but at that very instant it sank and immediately came up to the surface. The sailors, out of fear, lay still for a while and then let the boat float so that it came nearer the object which was carried by the current towards them. The monster suddenly turned his face and stared at the sailors who had now an opportunity of examining him narrowly. At last the sailors grew apprehensive of danger and began to retire, whereupon the monster blew his cheeks and made a sort of lowing noise and then dived under. The sailors declared upon oath that the monster appeared like an old man, with broad shoulders and strong-limbed. His

[1] See *Iceland, its Scenes and Sagas*, p. 349; Gould, l.c., pp. 506–507.

head was small in proportion to his body, and
he had short-curled, black hair which did not
reach below his ears; his eyes lay deep in his head,
and he had a meagre face, with a black beard;
from his waist downwards the merman was pointed
like a fish.[1]

Another story of a mermaid is told in *Voyage
towards the South Pole.*

A boat's crew were employed on Hall's Island,
and one of them, left to take care of some produce,
suddenly perceived an animal and heard its voice
which was rather musical. About ten o'clock, the
sailor, who had lain down, heard a noise resembling
human cries. As daylight in those latitudes never
disappears at this season, the sailor rose to see
what was the matter, but finding no one he went
to bed again. Presently he once more heard the
noise and rose up a second time, but still he saw
nothing. He conceived the possibility of a boat
being upset and of someone of the crew being in
distress, and he walked along the beach a few steps.
He now heard the noise more distinctly, but this
time in a musical strain. Searching round, the
sailor suddenly perceived an object lying on a rock
only a few yards away from him and the shore.
The sight of the strange creature upon which the
sailor was gazing frightened him. Its face and

---

[1] Pontoppidan, *Nat. Hist. of Norway*, p. 154; Gould, l.c., p.
508–509; Jones, l.c., p. 53.

shoulders were of human form and of a reddish colour and green hair hung over the shoulders. It had a tail which resembled that of a seal, but the extremities of the arms the sailor could not see distinctly. The creature continued to make the musical noise, but when it beheld the sailor it immediately disappeared. When the man saw his officers he told his story and affirmed on oath that he was speaking the truth. To confirm his statement, he made a cross on the sand and kissed it !

Another account of a mermaid is given in *The History of the Whales and Seals*, by Dr. R. Hamilton. A fishing-boat off one of the Shetland islands was reported to have caught a mermaid by its getting entangled in its lines. The animal, it was stated by those who had caught it, was about three feet long, and the upper part of the body resembled the human, with protuberant breasts, like a woman. The face, the forehead and neck were short, somewhat like that of a monkey. The arms, rather small, were kept folded across the breast, and the fingers were distinct, but not webbed. The inferior part of the body was that of a fish. The skin was smooth and of a grey colour. The animal was kept for three hours in the boat and several people had ample opportunity to examine it distinctly. They maintained that no gills were observed nor fins on either back or belly. The body was without scales or hair, was of silver-grey colour above and white

below, like that of the dogfish ; the breasts were about
as large as those of a woman ; the mouth and lips
were very distinct, and resembled the human.
The animal offered no resistance, nor attempted
to bite but uttered a low plaintive sound. The crew,
consisting of six Shetland fishermen, took it within
their boat, and none of them for a moment doubted
the fact that they had caught a mermaid.

Scottish fishermen are not afraid of a mermaid.
On the contrary, they are convinced that she is a
welcome guest and they only apprehend danger as the
result of bad treatment meted out to her. It was
this superstition which ultimately got the better of
curiosity. The sailors carefully disentangled the
creature from the lines and the hook which had
accidentally fastened in its body and gallantly returned it to its native element. It dived instantly
in a perpendicular direction.[1]

Many other curious details have come down to us
by tradition of mermaids being seen, of their appearance, and the evil results which attend their appearance. Thus in an Aberdeen Almanac for 1488, the
curious statement occurs :

Near the place where the Dee payeth its tribute
to the German Ocean, if curious observers of
wonderful things in nature will be pleased thither
to resort on the 1st, 13th, and 29th of May, and
in divers others times in the ensuing summer, as

[1] Gould, l.c., pp. 519–522.

also in the harvest time to the 7th and 14th of October, they will undoubtedly see a pretty company of mermaids, creatures of admirable beauty, and likewise hear their charming sweet melodious voices.[1]

With regard to the belief in mermen and mermaids Bishop Pontoppidan, in the famous 8th chapter of his *Natural History of Norway*, writes as follows :

" While we have no ground to believe in the various fables, yet, as to the existence of the creature, we may safely give our assent to it ; provided that it is not improbable or impossible in the nature of things, and that there is no want of confirmation from credible witnesses, and such as are not to be rejected. Both these propositions I shall show to be well grounded."

The author thereupon gives a minute and detailed description of the Norwegian mermen and mermaids and their young, called marmaete, or marmaele.

" If we enquire whether it be probable, that we should find in the Ocean a fish, or creature, which resembles the human species more than any other, it cannot be denied but we may answer in the affirmative, from the analogy and resemblance that is observed betwixt various species of land and sea-animals. It is well known there are sea-horses, sea-cows, sea-wolves, sea-hogs, sea-dogs, etc., which bear a near resemblance to the land-animals of those species."

[1] See Napier, *Folklore Record*, Vol. II, p. 106.

" There are several hundreds of persons in the
diocese of Bergen and in the Manor of Nordland,
persons of credit and reputation, who affirm, with
the strongest assurances, that they have seen this
kind of creature sometimes at a distance, and at
other times quite close to their boats, standing
upright and formed like a human creature down to
the middle ; the rest they could not see." In 1719,
the Reverend Peter Angel, along with several other
inhabitants of Alstahong in Nordland, saw a merman
lying dead on a point of land near the sea which had
been cast ashore by the waves, along with several
sea-calves, and other dead fish. The length of this
creature was much greater than what has been
mentioned of any before, namely above three
fathoms. It was of dark grey colour all over ; in
the lower part it was like a fish, and had a tail like
a porpoise. The face resembled that of a man,
with a mouth, forehead, eyes, etc. The nose was
flat, and, as it were, pressed down to the face, in
which the nostrils have ever been visible. The
breast was not far from the head ; the arms seemed
to hang to the side, to which they were joined by a
thin skin or membrane. The hands were to appearance like the paws of a sea-calf. The back of this
creature was very fat, and a great part of it was cut
off, which, with the liver, yielded a large quantity
of train oil . . .

" The latest instance I have learned of a

merman's being seen was in Denmark; and this stands attested so well that it deserves to be quoted after all the others. In 1723, on the 20th of September, the burgomaster of Elseneur examined three ferrymen about a sea-monster which these ferrymen affirmed they had seen a few weeks before. It appeared that about two months before the ferrymen were towing a ship just arrived from the Baltic, and which was then under full sail. At a distance of an English mile they observed something floating on the water like a dead body, which made them row to it, that they might see what it was. It turned out to be a merman.

" The before-mentioned Marmaele," continues Bishop Pontoppidan, " or, as some call it, Marmaete, belongs also to this class of the mermaid; though I shall not call it the merman's offspring, yet one might give it this name till further examined into. This creature is often caught on hooks, and is well-known to most fishermen. They are of different sizes; some are of the bigness of an infant of half a year old; others of one of a year; and others again as big as a child of three years old: of this last size there was one lately taken in Selloe Soogn; the upper part was like a child, but the rest like a fish. Those who caught it threw it directly into the sea. Sometimes the peasants take them home to their houses, and, as they say, give them milk, which they drink. They tell us that these creatures then roll their eyes about strangely, as if it was out of curiosity, or surprise, to see what they had not seen before. Those that venture to take them home, do it in hopes of having something foretold by them ; but they do not keep them above twenty-four hours, superstitiously thinking themselves bound to row out to sea, and put them down in the same place where they found them."

While Bishop Pontoppidan does not deny the existence of the merman, he refuses to add credence to the many fables and legends clustering round the mermen and the sirens.

" The existence of this creature," he writes, " is questioned by many, nor is it at all to be wondered at, because most of the accounts we have had of it are mixed with mere fables, and may be looked upon as idle tales. Such is the story of a merman, taken by the fishermen at Nordeland, near Bergen ; which, they say, sung an unmusical song. Such is also the account of a mermaid that called herself Isbrandt, and held several conversations with a peasant at Samsoc ; in which she foretold the birth of Christian IV, and made the peasant preach repentance to the courtiers of Frederick II who were very much given to drunkenness.

" According to another account two senators, on their return from Norway to Denmark, caught such a merman, but were obliged to let him go into the water again. Whilst he lay upon the deck, he spoke Danish to them and threatened if they did not give him his liberty, that the ship should be cast away, and every soul of the crew should perish."

" This," adds Pontoppidan, " is as idle as the other stories. When such fictions are mixed with the history of the merman, and when that creature is represented as a prophet and an orator ; when they give the mermaid a melodious voice, and tell us that she is a fine singer ; one need not wonder that so few people of sense will give credit to such absurdities ; or that they even doubt the existence of such a creature.[1]

In the " Nibelungenlied " it is told how the hero Hagen, searching up and down on the banks of the river, saw wise women bathing in a fountain. He seized their clothes, although he did them no further harm. Thereupon one of the merwives, Hadebure by name, thus spoke to Hagen :

" Noble knight Hagen, if you will give us back our clothes, we will make known to you how ye shall accomplish your journey to the Court of the Huns."

As she spoke, they floated like the birds before him on the flood. The merwife told Hagen that they may well go to Etzel's land, for never heroes reached such honour as they will. Hagen gave the merwives back their wonderful apparel, and

[1] Erick Pontoppidan, *The Natural History of Norway*, London, 1755, Vol. II, pp. 186–195.

MERMEN AND MERMAIDS FOLLOWING A VESSEL

they told him the way to Etzel's Court. Thereupon the other merwife, who was called Sigelint, warned Hagen that her companion for love of her clothes had lied to him, and if he goes to the Huns then he will be sore deceived. Hagen tells the merwives that they are deceiving him, for they cannot all remain dead in Hunland, to which one of the merwives replied that the King's chaplain alone will return in safety. Hagen refused to take council and asked the merwives to show him over the water.[1]

The superstition that mermaids were anxious to decoy mortals to destruction has been illustrated by Leyden in his poem, " The Mermaid."

> Thus, all to soothe the chieftain's woe,
> Far from the maid he loved so dear,
> The song arose, so soft and slow,
> He seem'd her prating sigh to hear.
>
> That sea-maid's form of pearly light,
> Was whiter than the downy spray,
> And round her bosom, heaving bright,
> Her glossy, yellow ringlets play.
>
> Born on a foaming crested wave
> She reached amain the bounding prow,
> Then clasping fast the cheftain brave,
> She, plunging, sought the deep below.
>
> SIR WALTER SCOTT,
> *Minstrelsy of the Scottish Border.*

A curious custom, which no doubt originated in this superstition, existed in the Isle of Man. Once

[1] J. M. Ludlow, *Popular Epics of the Middle Ages,* 1865, Vol. I, p. 134.

upon a time, so the tradition runs, a mermaid of uncommon beauty had exerted such an influence over the male population that she induced numbers of them, by the enchantment of her sweet voice, to follow her footsteps and thus by degrees led them into the sea where they perished.

This exercise of power of the bewitching sea-maiden had continued for a long time and great apprehension as for the future of the island pre-vailed. One day, however, a knight-errant sprang up who discovered a means of counteracting the charms of the siren. The latter evaded destruction by taking the form of a wren, but a spell was cast upon her and she was condemned to reanimate the same form on every succeeding New Year's Day, with the definite sentence that she must ultimately perish by human hand. On the specified anni-versary, therefore, efforts were made to annihilate the sea-maid and the wrens were pursued, fired at and destroyed without mercy. Their feathers were preserved as a charm against shipwreck for one year. Boys now keep up the old custom for amusement.[1]

Kelpies, Fairies, and Water-Sprites.

The belief in fairies, water-sprites, and kelpies was very common in olden times among sailors, and still clings to the minds of the seafaring com-

[1] See *British Popular Customs*, pp. 494–495 ; T. F. Thiselton Dyer, *Folklore of Shakespeare*, 1883, p. 470.

munity. These genii, often malignant, were believed
to allure women and children to their subaqueous
haunts where they devoured them. Hapless travellers, too, and mariners had to suffer from the
kelpies and water-sprites. Swelling the torrents,
the malignant sprites caused many a disaster.
Traditions and folk-tales of water-spirits still linger
on the coasts of Scotland and France, and elsewhere.

The kelpie was believed to be a creature living
mostly in deep pools of rivers and streams, and
commonly appeared as a black horse. He often
approached the traveller, inducing the latter to
mount him, whereupon he rushed to his pool
carrying off the victim to his death. There is a
tradition among French fishermen of Dieppe that
at a certain season of the year the water-fairies hold
a bazaar on the cliffs overhanging the sea. Here
they exhibit wares of rare beauty, offering them
for sale. The passing fisherman who is strong
enough to resist the temptation and the allurements
and to turn away his head from the strange beings,
who employ every art of fascination, escapes un-
harmed. But woe to him who is persuaded to
approach the brilliant spectacle, for he is gradually
drawn to the edge of the cliff and hurled into the
waves.

FOLK-TALES OF MERMEN AND MERMAIDS

Yet still I yearn to hear from out the gloom
Of some high cavern shadowing o'er the bay,
Where a wild echo sobbeth night and day
And 'mid sharp rocks the crystal waters boom,
Sound of sea-Mirth into the sunlight stream,
And songs and laughter thrill the summer air
And glimpse the Gods in festal robes, and dream
That they are merry with the Nereids there.

Still do I yearn to see Poseidon urge
His wheels along the waves and hear the snort
Of his horn'd horses panting into port
Over the neck of some great frowning surge.
Still do I yearn with mortal ears to hear
The noonday Triton sound his rosy shell
'Mid these cool rocks, and see the dolphins rear
Their pearly flanks, enchanted by the spell.

Behind this cape of breezy bowers we'll stand,
If haply we may hear the charming song
Of lorn Arion as he glides along
Between the mossy headlands harp in hand,
Wondering with wild blue eyes and hair astray—
Or watch the laughing Galatea whirl
Past us into the green and purple bay
Tilted in sea green scarf and ribbed pearl.

See'st thou yon grot ?—'tis paved with golden grain—
There the blue waters resting from their play
Sleep through the August noon, and day by day
A white-arm'd Sea-nymph with her fair-hair'd train
Cleaves the calm flood serene as mountain springs
With her white arms, and soon a sparry cave
Trembles with all its tears the while she sings
Looking towards the windless azure wave.

There in clear gloom she muses far away
From her bright-eyed companions, there she weaves
A coronal of gems and wild sea-leaves,
A fairy wreath against her bridal day,
Singing and looking seaward with soft eyes,
That her young God may see her from the water.
And in the light of rainbows may arise
And clasp unto his heart the Ocean daughter.

I heard that song far down along the sea,
Its silver sweetness on the breezes flew
Like wafted odours or clear drops of dew
Freshening the Morn, and rose above the roar
Of tumbling waves and murmuring ripplets clear,
And when it ceased I could have dived far under
The green and purple deeps again to hear
That charming song and see that Ocean wonder.

A. TENNYSON.

CHAPTER VIII

FOLK-TALES OF MERMEN AND MERMAIDS

Legends and folk-tales in the Shetland Islands—The mermen and merwomen of Assens—The councillors of Christian IV of Denmark capture a merman—The merwife of Tribirke—The girdle with precious stones—The bull throwing up the earth with his horns—The deceived peasants—The inhabitants of Jupille and the three mysterious damsels—A dance till midnight—The pledge of love—The lovesick youth—The fisherman from St. Jacut and the sea-fairies—The magic ointment—The clairvoyant fisherman—The merman who married the daughter of a poor fisherman—A longing for church—The merman in despair—Sadko, the Novgorod trader—The mermaid who forgot her sealskin—The enamoured Shetlander—The return to the watery home—The sea-woman of Harlem—The fisherman and the mysterious hand—" To-night they dance at Kennare "—The fisherman gunner—The avenging wave—The fisherman changed into a whale—The lady of Collrus—The castle of Loholm and its story—The sea-maiden and the fisherman—The mermaid of Saundersfoot—The poor labouring man and the generous mermaid.

NUMEROUS tales connected with mermaids exist in the Shetland Islands. They are said to dwell in the sea among the fishes, in habitations of pearl and coral. They resemble human beings but greatly exceed them in beauty. When they wish to visit the upper world they put on the garb of some fish, but woe to those who lose this garb, for then all their hopes of returning to the depth of the ocean are annihilated and they are obliged to stay where they are. The sacred wells are a very favourite place with the fair children of the sea. Here, undisturbed by men, the green-haired beauties of the ocean lay aside their garb and revel in the clear moonlight. They are mortal, and are often, on their excursions, exposed to dangers, for examples are not wanting of their having been taken by fishermen and killed. It often happens that earthly men get mermaids into their power and marry them.[1]

Several stories of mermaids are related by Thorpe.

In the neighbourhood of Assens there once appeared an incredible number of mermen and mer-women on the strand. Aged fishermen relate how they often and often have seen the merwives sitting there on large stones out in the water, with children at the breast, which they quickly thrust on their backs when, terrified at the approach of man, they darted down into the water. It is further related that in those places sea-cows and sea-bulls have been seen to land in the fields, seeking intercourse with other cattle.

In the year 1619 King Christian IV sent two of his councillors, Oluf Rosenspar and Christian Holck, to Norway, there to hold a Diet. On their return they captured a merman. In form this merman resembled a man. For a long time he rolled himself backwards and forwards, but at length lay as if he were dead. On one of the bystanders saying to him :

[1] See Faye, pp. 60, 61 ; Thorpe, II, p. 73.

" It must indeed be a wonderful God that has such human creatures also in the water,"

" Yes," he replied : " if thou knowest that as well as I, then mightest thou say so. But if ye do not instantly restore me to the water, neither the ship nor yourselves shall ever reach land." After this he would not utter a word, but was placed in the boat, and thence sprang into the water.[1]

Another story runs as follows : Out in Nord-strand there dwells a merwife who once drove her cattle up on the seashore and let them graze the whole day on Tribirke Mark. This did not at all please the peasantry thereabouts, who for ages have been notorious for their coveteousness ; they therefore took measures for intercepting the cattle, whereby they succeeded in driving the merwife with all her herd into an enclosure near the town, from which they would not allow her to escape until she had paid them for pasturage on their lands. Having assured them that she had no money to give, they required her to give them the girdle she wore round her body, which appeared very costly and shone as with precious stones. There being no alternative, she redeemed herself and cattle by giving them the girdle. But as she was driving her cattle down to the shore, she said to her large bull : " Rake up now ! " Whereupon the animal began to throw up the earth with his horns and to cast up

[1] Thorpe, II, p. 170.

the sand along the sea-coast; and as the wind now blew from the north-west, the sand was drifted in over the country towards the village of Tribirke, so that the church was nearly buried under it. Of the costly girdle, too, they had but a shortlived gratification, for on returning home and examining it more closely, it was found to consist of worthless rushes.[1]

One autumn evening as the joyful inhabitants of Jupille, at the end of the vintage, were springing about and dancing on the verdant turf, three damsels suddenly approached them from the banks of the Meuse, and joined the mirthful assemblage. They were attired in garments of dazzling whiteness, and on their fair locks were garlands of fresh-blown water-lilies. Whether they walked or only glided on the earth no one could say. The young lads of Jupille had never met with such light dancers.

When the dancing was over, all sat down in a circle, and the three damsels began to sing, and that with such sweet voice that the eyes of all were fixed on them, and no one thought how far the night was already advanced. To their surprise the clock struck the hour of midnight, when the damsels, after whispering a few words together, greeted the company round and disappeared.

On the following evening, just as the moon was risen, they returned, when the young men instantly hastened up to them, requesting them to dance.

[1] Thorpe, l.c., II, p. 171.

As the night was sultry, one of them drew off her gloves which her partner took charge of. This time the clock struck twelve while they were still engaged in the dance. Terrified at the sound the damsels started and were hastening away, when one exclaimed : " Where are my gloves ? " But the youth would not restore them, retaining them as a pledge of love ; and the damsel with her companions hurried away without them. Her partner followed with equal speed, being but too desirous of discovering where the beauteous maiden dwelt. They proceeded on and on, when, on reaching the Meuse, the damsels sprang into the water and vanished. When on the following morning the love-sick youth revisited the spot, the water was blood-red. The maidens never appeared again.[1]

To arouse the anger of mermaids is dangerous, and the sea-ladies never fail to take their revenge.

A fisherman from St. Jacut was the last to return home one evening, at dusk, from the scene of his labours. As he walked along the wet sand of the seashore he suddenly came upon a number of sea-fairies in a cavern, talking and gesticulating with vivacity, though he could not hear what they said. He beheld them rub their eyes and bodies with a sort of ointment, when suddenly their appearance changed, and they were enabled to walk away in the guise of ordinary women. The fisherman

[1] Thorpe, III, pp. 199-200.

concealed himself behind a large rock and watched the sea-fairies out of sight. When they had all disappeared, he made straight for the cave. Here he found what was left of the ointment and taking a little on his finger rubbed it around his left eye.

To his great surprise he found himself able to penetrate the disguises assumed by the fairies for the purpose of robbing or annoying mankind. The fisherman now recognized as one of the fairies a beggar-woman whom he saw a few days afterwards going from door to door and begging for charity. He saw her also casting spells on certain houses and peering eagerly into them as if looking for something to steal. When he was out in his boat the fisherman had now acquired the ability to distinguish between real fish and fish which were only in reality ladies of the sea in disguise who were busy entangling nets or playing tricks upon seamen.

One day the fisherman attended the fair of Plombalay, where he saw several elves who had taken the disguise of showmen and fortune-tellers and were deceiving the countryfolk. The fisherman kept clear of their temptations, smiling to himself at what he saw. Suddenly some of the elves surprised his smile and by the look of anger in their eyes the fisherman knew that they had guessed his secret. Before he had time to fly, one of the elves struck his clairvoyant eye with a stick and burst it. That is

what happened to him who tried to learn the secrets
of the ladies of the sea.[1]

The following tale of a merman who married a
mortal maid is told by Thorpe :

In the diocese of Aarhuus there once dwelt two
poor people who had an only daughter named
Margaret, or Grethe. One day, when she had
been sent down to the seaside to fetch sand and
was scooping it into her apron, a merman rose
from the water. His beard was greener than the
salt sea, he was of comely aspect, and spoke in
friendly words to the girl, saying :

" Follow me, Grethe. I will give thee as much
silver as thy heart can desire."

" That would not be amiss," answered she,
" for we have not much of that article at home."

So she suffered herself to be enticed, and he took
her by the hand and conducted her to the bottom of
the ocean where she became mother of five children.

After a lapse of time, and when she had nearly
forgotten her Christian belief, as she was sitting
one holiday morning, rocking her youngest child
in her lap, she heard the church bells ringing above
her, and was seized with a strong fit of melancholy
and longing after church ; and as she sat and sighed
with the tears rolling down her cheeks, the merman
observing her sorrow, enquired the cause of it.
She then besought him earnestly, with many

[1] Sébillot, *Litt. orale ;* see *Folklore,* I, pp. 211-212.

expressions of affection, to allow her once more to go to church. The merman could not withstand her affliction, but conducted her up to land, repeatedly exhorting her to return quickly to her children. In the middle of the sermon the merman came outside of the church and cried :

" Grethe, Grethe ! "

She heard him plainly enough, but resolved within herself that she would stay and hear the sermon out. When the sermon was ended the merman came a second time to the church, crying : " Grethe ! Grethe ! art thou soon coming ? Thy children are longing after thee ! " On finding that she did not come, he began to weep bitterly, and again descended to the bottom of the sea. But from that time Grethe continued with her parents, and let the merman himself take care of the poor little children. His wail and lamentations are often to be heard from the deep.[1]

Numerous stories of watermen and watermaids are told in Russian folklore, where the nymphs are known as the *roussalki* and the water-king as the Tsar Morskoi.

The following story of a Novgorod trader named Sadko is a good specimen. One day, feeling rather dreary on account of his great poverty, he went down to the shore of the lake Leman and there began to play on his musical instrument, the *gusli*.

[1] Thorpe, II, p. 172.

Suddenly the waters of the lake were troubled and up rose the water-king, the Tsar Morskoi, who thanked the trader for his pleasant music and promised him a reward. Sadko thereupon threw a net into the lake and drew a great treasure.

He had now become a very wealthy merchant, and one day he was sailing over the blue sea when suddenly the vessel stopped and could proceed no farther. The sailors wondered on account of whose guilt their vessel had been stopped and decided to cast lots. The lot fell on Sadko, who now confessed that he had been sailing on the sea for twelve years, but had forgotten to pay tribute to the Tsar Morskoi or king of the waters. The sailors thereupon flung Sadko into the sea and their vessel could now move on. When Sadko sank to the bottom of the sea, he found a dwelling made of wood where lay the Tsar Morskoi.

" I have been expecting thee for twelve years," said the water-king, " and am anxious to hear thee play. Begin at once."

Sadko obeyed and the water-king was greatly pleased with his music. The Tsar Morskoi was so pleased with Sadko that as a reward he offered him the hand of any of his thirty daughters. Sadko chose the nymph Volkhof and was married to her.

The belief in mermen and mermaids has not yet died out among seafaring people and sailors. Numerous legends and tales are current among

the inhabitants on the seashore. One of these
stories told in the Shetland Islands runs as follows :

One day a man walking along the sand perceived
a group of mermen and mermaids dancing in the
moonlight. Their sealskins which they usually
wear, and which enable them to live in the depths
of the water, were lying in a heap near by. The
dance over, the mermen and mermaids each picked
up his or her sealskin and disappeared in the sea.
One of these supernatural beings had, however,
evidently forgotten the sealskin in the hurry. The
Shetlander found it and hid it. When he returned
to the seashore his eyes were dazzled by the supernatural beauty of a maid who was sitting on the
beach lamenting the loss of her sealskin. Without
this charm it was impossible for her to return to her
watery home and she was doomed to remain an
exile on land. Never had the Shetlander gazed
upon such loveliness and beauty, and he fell madly
in love with the beautiful mermaid. The latter
implored the mortal man to return to her the talisman he had found, but her tears and entreaties
were of no avail, for the lover proved inexorable.

" Abide with me," he pleaded, " under my roof,
as my wife. I will cherish and make thee forget
thy wet and dark home."

For a long time the mermaid pleaded and begged
her lover to allow her to return to her own people,
but at last, seeing that there was no alternative,

she yielded to the Shetlander's desire. The two were duly married and several children were born to them. The passion and love of the husband were, however, not returned by the wife, who was constantly yearning for her home at the bottom of the sea.

Many a time and oft did the mermaid wander at the seashore or sit down on the beach, and with longing eyes gaze upon the wide expanse of water. Sometimes, at a signal from her, someone would appear upon the surface of the water and the two would converse in an unknown tongue. Years went by and neither the love of the husband nor the coldness of the beautiful maid from the watery deep had diminished. The mother was evidently fond of her children, but she was ready to run away and return to her original home at the first opportunity. Soon such an opportunity was offered to her and she seized it at once. One day, one of her boys found the sealskin his father had hidden away so securely under a mill-wheel and brought the find to his mother. With a start of joy the exiled mermaid exclaimed : " My sealskin, at last ! "

The temptation to return to her own people was stronger even than her love for the boy whom she kissed fondly, for she was now about to leave him for ever.

" Good-bye," she cried, and speedily ran across the sands.

At that moment the husband, seeing his wife

running on the beach carrying the sealskin, guessed the truth. He hurried after her to stop her, but it was too late. He saw the mother of his children transformed in the shape of the seal, and diving into the sea.[1]

The famous story of the sea-woman of Harlem has often been told.

There was a great tempest at sea and the high tides flooded many villages in Holland and Friesland, and drowned many people. Now during that tempest there came a sea-woman swimming in Zuyderzee between the town of Campen and Edam and entered into the straight of a broken dyke in the Purmermer, where she remained for a long time. The hole by which she had entered having been stopped as soon as the storm had abated, the woman could not return to the sea. She was discovered by some women who were daily going to the pastures to milk their cows. Afraid at first of the creature, their curiosity had the upper hand at last, and rowing in a boat towards the sea-woman, they drew her out of the water by force and carried her to the town of Edam. Here the mermaid was washed and cleansed and apparelled, and was like any other woman. She disliked her captivity and often tried to escape, but she was watched and guarded very carefully. She gradually accustomed herself to her new life, to the food of the land-people,

[1] Jones, l.c., pp. 22–23.

learned to spin and always paid great reverence to the sign of the cross. Many people came to see her from far, and the people of Harlem persuaded the inhabitants of Edam to let them have the strange creature. She lived in Harlem for fifteen years and was buried in the churchyard on account of the reverence she had always paid to the cross.

One of the characteristics of the mermen and mermaids is their lack of a soul, and in all the tales current about them they are represented as yearning for one. One day a mermaid visited a Scottish peasant who was reading his Bible and asked him whether it was written in his Sacred Book that she too would find salvation. When the peasant replied in the negative, the mermaid uttered a shriek and, loudly weeping, disappeared. Here, of course, we have the motif of the famous story of Undine, by Baron de la Motte Fouqué.

This explains the reason of the love of mermaids for mortal men. There is a story of a mermaid who once stopped a vessel which had a queen on board, and made the latter promise that she would give the subaqueous beauty one of her sons. The vessel was allowed to proceed on its voyage, but one day when the prince was riding along the seashore, his horse suddenly plunged into the water and carried him to the palace of the mermaid. Here he remained for a long time, and when at last he returned to earth the lady followed him.

Numerous are the stories and tales of mermaids current in the North Sea and in the northern countries.

One night, so runs a story, Swedish fishermen were sleeping in their wooden huts when the door suddenly opened and one of the fishermen who was awake saw a woman's white hand. He related this incident to his friends the next day, and a reckless young fellow exclaimed :

" Why on earth did you not seize the hand and lay hold on the woman ? To-night I will lay awake and wait for the woman."

When the hand again appeared through the open door the fisherman seized it, but he was drawn through the door and disappeared. Nothing was heard of him for years, and his wife remarried. Years afterwards the young man turned up again and he told how he had been drawn by a mermaid whose hand he had seized and had been compelled to remain with her in her subaqueous palace.

One day she said to him : " To-night the dance at Kennare," which was the native place of the fisherman. " Your wife is remarried and you can go up and see her in her bridal wreath, but beware of entering beneath the roof." The fisherman went ashore and for some time stood there looking at the festival, but unable to resist any longer, he entered. The roof of the farm buildings was carried off that night and the fisherman died three days afterwards.

The mermaids are supposed to heap favours

upon those to whom they happen to have taken a
fancy, but woe to those who despise their favours.
Thus Duke Magnus, son of Gustavus Vasa, was
visited by a fair and lovely mermaid who promised
him love and treasure if he would only take her to
wife. Prince Magnus refused and he died insane.

One day a fisherman, named Gunnar, was saved
from drowning by a mermaid and out of gratitude
he promised to visit the maiden once a week. He
kept his promise, but one day when he failed to
keep his appointment the surging sea sent its roaring
waves over the beach and into the village where the
fisherman dwelt and carried away house and inmates
to the bottom of the sea.

On the western coast of Ireland the fishermen
used to explain the rare conjunctions of wind and
tide which occurred only in one bay, as follows :
The origin of the " avenging wave " was the work
of an offended mermaid. A fisherman of the name
of Shea had once killed a mermaid, although she had
begged him to have mercy on her. When next the
fisherman sailed on the bay the waves arose in all
their fury, and the fisherman, struck by his guilty
conscience, fled in terror. The avenging waves
overtook him and he and all those who were in his
boats perished, and every time when one of the
fisherman's descendants appears in the bay the
avenging waves arise.

Another story tells of a sailor who had lived with

a mermaid and in time forsaken her. She changed
him into a whale and he killed many men and destroyed many ships until one day a priest whose
daughter the enchanted fisherman had swallowed,
allured, by means of charms, the whale to the seashore where it died.

One day an Irishman named Fitzgerald caught
a Merrow, as the mermaid is called in Ireland,
with her enchanted cap, or *cohulfeen drinth*, lying on
the rock near by. He took hold of the cap and thus
could possess himself of the maiden who did not
seem to be averse to a union with mortal man.
The pair were married and lived happily together
for many years and many children were born to them.
One day the Lady of Collrus, as the mermaid was
now called, discovered in a corner of her house her
cap. She now remembered her father the king and
her mother the queen in their splendid subaqueous
palace, and a longing awoke in her heart to visit
once more the scenes of her childhood. She had
no intention whatever to forsake her husband or
children, but simply to pay a visit to her home
under the waters. She kissed her children and
went down to the beach. As soon, however, as the
cap was on her head, the remembrance of her life
on earth fled from her and she forgot all about her
husband and children. She plunged into the sea and
never returned.

A Swedish legend runs as follows :

In West Gothland, in the district of Biärke, there is a lake with beautifully wooded shores, called Anten. On an isle in this lake there was formerly an ancient castle, remains of which are still to be seen, called Loholm, in which dwelt Sir Gunnar, a renowned knight, and ancestor of the famous family of Leionhutvud, of Lewenhapt. Once, when out on the lake he had fallen into danger, a merwife came to his aid, but exacted from him the promise, that on a certain day he should meet her again at the same place. One Thursday evening she sat expecting the knight; but he forgot his promise. She then caused the water of the lake to swell over Loholm, until Sir Gunnar was forced to take refuge in a higher apartment; but the water reached even that. He then sought safety in the drawbridge tower, but there the billows again overtook him. He next committed himself to a boat, which sank near a large stone called to this day Gunnar's stone; from which time Sir Gunnar, it is said, lives constantly with his merwife. When fishermen or the country people row by the stone, they usually lift their hats, as a salutation to Sir Gunnar, in the belief that if they neglected to do so they would have no success. From that time no one dwelt in Loholm, of the materials of which was built the noble castle of Gräfnäess, on a peninsula in the same lake, with tower-ditches, and drawbridges, remains of which are still visible. From this Sir

Gunnar descended Erik Abrahamsson, father-in-law
of Gustavus the First.[1]

There is a long story in Campbell's *Tales of the
West Highlands*, entitled " The sea-maiden."

It tells of a poor old fisherman, who was out
fishing, but was not getting much fish. Now a
sea-maiden rose at the side of his boat and asked
him if he was getting fish. The old man answered
that he was not. They had a long talk, and the
sea-maiden made a bargain with the old fisherman.
She promised him plenty of fish for his first son.

" But I have none," said the fisherman.

" You will have three sons," replied the sea-maiden.

Then she gave him three grains for his wife, three
grains for his dog and three grains for his mare.

" Thou wilt have three sons," said the sea-maiden,
" and when thy son is three years old thou wilt bring
him to me. And now thou wilt have plenty of fish."

The sea-maiden disappeared, and everything
happened as she had said. The old fisherman was
allowed to keep his son until he was eighteen, but
in the end he was compelled to tell his son of the
bargain he had made with the sea-maiden.

" Oh," said the lad, " I will go to a place where
there is not a drop of salt water." He mounted one
of his horses and went away. On his way he rendered a service to a lion, a wolf and a falcon, and the
grateful beasts promised him to be at his side

[1] Thorpe, l.c., Vol. II, p. 77.

whenever he was in need. According to another version the three beasts were a dog, a falcon and an otter.

The lad went on his way and became a king's herd.

He came to grips several times with wild giants and every time the grateful beasts, faithful to their promise, hurried to his assistance. One day when he came home there was sorrow in the king's house, for a great beast with three heads had come from the sea and someone had to be eaten. The lot had fallen this time on the king's daughter. The herd killed the monster, saved the king's daughter, and married her. But one day he went to the seashore and the sea-maiden came out and took the lad. The king's daughter was sorrowful, went to the soothsayer and learned what to do.

She took her harp and went to the seashore and played, and the sea-maiden came up to listen, for sea-maidens are fonder of music than any other creatures. And when the king's daughter saw the sea-maiden she stopped playing. The sea-maiden said :

" Play on," but the king's daughter said : " Not till I see my man again."

Then the sea-maiden put up his head. The king's daughter played again, and stopped, and then the sea-maiden put him up to the waist. Then the king's daughter played again and stopped, and the sea-maiden placed him on her palm. The lad immediately thought of the falcon, and he became

one and flew on shore. But the sea-maiden took
the wife. With the help, however, of the grateful
beasts the fisherman's son got hold of the soul of
the sea-maiden and she died.[1]

The following story of the Mermaid of Saundersfoot is told by Karl Blind.

A mermaid was once left high and dry on a large
rock off Saundersfoot, a small seaside village near
Tenby; and there she sat, with her glass and
comb, combing her hair, which was the colour of
the sea, of greenish hue—and bewailing her fate,
as she had no means of getting to the sea. A poor
labouring man, coming down to the beach to gather
mussels, caught sight of her, and him she at once
asked to have pity on her and carry her out to the
water. In return she promised him money, which she
knew well where to find. He carried her from the
rock, and put her into the sea; and the next day she
came back, bringing with her silver and gold, *all
of which she had found at the bottom of the sea.* Day
by day the poor labouring man would come down
to the rock, and taking the mermaid's gifts, would
often repay them by the same service she had at
first asked him for. And the man became wonder-
fully rich, and the people in the neighbourhood
gave the rock the name of the Mermaid's Rock, a
name which has clung to it ever since.[2]

[1] See Campbell, *Tales of the Highlands,* Vol. I, p. 71; see also
Koehler, *Kleine Schriften.*
[2] *Gentleman's Magazine,* 1882, Vol. CCLII, p. 476.

SEA-MONSTERS

CHAPTER IX

SEA-MONSTERS

Lively imagination of mariners—The Kraken—Aristotle and
Pliny—Scandinavia, the classic land of superstitions—Olaus
Magnus on the Kraken—Eric Falkendorff's letter to Pope
Leon—Mass read on a mysterious island—A physician of
Eisenach—Hans Egede's description of a sea-monster—The
sea-monster called Hafgufa—The sea-monster called Drew—
Pontoppidan's description of the Kraken—Floating islands—
A fabulous romance—Gummer's Ore—The dimensions of the
whale—A gigantic whale in the Straits of Gibraltar—A sea-
monster in the Elbe—Folk-tales in the Talmud—The Leviathan—The adventures of Rabbi bar bar Hanah—A gigantic
fish taken for an island—A folk-tale of the Leviathan—The
lad who cast his bread upon the waters—The big fish—The
lad who was taught seventy languages—The two ravens—
The treasure of King Solomon—The barnacle—Gerard's
description of the barnacle.

THE bottom of the sea has always been
supposed to harbour monsters of every
kind and description, and it is quite natural
that seafaring people and mariners, having on many
occasions perceived gigantic fishes, should with their
lively imagination have exaggerated and given rise
to many fables and superstitions.

The stories about the Kraken, that fabulous sea-
monster, can be traced back to Aristotle and Pliny,
but it is Scandinavia which became the classic land
of the superstitions and fables concerning the Kraken
with all its horrors and terrors.

Olaus Magnus, the last Catholic bishop of Sweden, writes in 1555 that the sea-monster had a skin resembling the gravel on the seashore which fact induced seafaring men to take its back sometimes for an island, to land on it, to light a fire, and suddenly, when the monster began to move, to be compelled to run for their lives.

Eric Falkendorff, Bishop of Nidros, wrote in 1520 to Pope Leon a long letter on the subject of the sea-monster. Sunday, when the bishop was at sea, he greatly regretted his inability to celebrate mass on land with all the required solemnity. Suddenly there emerged from the waves an island, and the bishop was able to land on it and celebrate mass. Scarcely, however, had he left this mysterious island and returned on board his ship when it vanished.

In 1700 a physician in Eisenach, Christian Paullinus, and a Dane, Bartholinus, relate of the Kraken. The latter had been able to celebrate mass on its back.

Hans Egede, in his description of Groenland, speaks of another sea-monster.

" The third monster," writes Egede, quoting from Tormader's *History of Groenland*, " named Hafgufa, is so terrible and frightful that the author does not well know how to describe it, and no wonder, because he never had any true relation of it ; its shape, length and bulk seem to exceed all size and measure. They that pretend to have seen it, say that it appeared to them more like a land than a fish, or sea-animal. And as there never has been seen above two of them in the wide open sea, they conclude that there can be no breed of them ; for if they should breed, or multiply, all the rest of fishes must be destroyed at last, their vast body wanting such large quantities of nourishment. When the monster is hungry, it is said to void through the mouth some matter of a sweet scent, which perfumes the whole sea ; and by this means it allures and draws all sorts of fishes and animals, even the whales, to it. They flock thither and run into the wide opened swallow of the hideous monster, as into a whirlpool, till its belly is well freighted with a copious load of all sorts of fishes and then it shuts the swallow, and has for the whole year enough to digest and to live upon ; for it is said to make but one large meal a year."

Fishermen also tell a tale of another monster. They say that a great ghostly sea-monster now and then appears in the main sea, which they call Kraken, and is no doubt the same that the Islanders call Hafgufa. They say that its body reaches several miles in length, and that it is most seen in a calm. When it comes out of the water, it seems to cover the whole surface of the sea. All sorts of fishes flock together upon it, as upon a bank of the sea, and that many fishing-boats come thither to catch fish, not suspecting that they lie upon such a dreadful monster. This they at last understand by the entangling of their hooks and angles in its body. The monster, feeling the latter, rises softly from the bottom to the surface and seizes them all. They can, however, easily avoid their destruction, as they only have to call it by its name, which it no sooner hears but it sinks down again as softly as it did rise.

Another sea-monster, which seamen and fishermen call the Drew, keeps no constant shape or figure, but now appears in one, now in another. It appears and is heard before any misfortunes, as shipwrecks and the like, happen at sea, which it forebodes with a most frightful and ghostly howling.[1]

With regard to the Kraken, Bishop Pontoppidan writes as follows :

" Many authors speak of certain islands which suddenly appear and as suddenly vanish. This was a thing nobody could comprehend ; so that one ought not to wonder at the common people, and even those that were a degree above them, for looking upon those moving islands to be inhabited by evil spirits, which appeared sometimes in such places where the seamen, by daily experience, knew very well that there was no such thing as a rock, much less an island. They often, however, found something at sea which had the appearance of land, and consequently were confounded, made false

---

[1] Hans Egede, *The Natural History of Groenland*, p. 86-88.

SEA MONSTER

reckonings, and were taken out of their course, and brought into the greater inconveniences.

Many seafaring people give accounts of such appearances of land, and their suddenly vanishing away, and particularly here in the North Sea. These islands, in the boisterous ocean, cannot be imagined to be in the nature of those real floating islands, that are seen on stagnated waters, and which are found in Norway and in other places. These could not possibly hold or stand against the violence of the waves in the ocean, which break the largest vessels. Our sailors have, therefore, concluded that this delusion could come from no other than the great deceiver, the devil. But I think that we ought not to charge this apostate spirit without cause. I rather believe that this devil who so suddenly makes and unmakes these floating islands is nothing else but the Kraken, which some seafaring people call Sol-draulen, or sea-mischief.

"What the credulous Olaus Magnus writes of the whole being so large, that his back is looked upon as an island ; and that people might land, light fires and do various kinds of works upon it, is a notoriously fabulous and ridiculous romance."

The author then quotes an incident we have referred to above with regard to Gummer's Ore. "Amongst the rocks about Stockholm there is sometimes seen a certain tract of land which at other times disappears, and is seen again in another place.

Buraeus had placed this as an island in his map. The peasants say that it is not always seen, and that it lies out in the open sea. Now Baron Grippenhielm related that one Sunday, when he was out among the rocks, he saw something like three points of land in the sea, which surprised him a little. He called a peasant to enquire for Gummer's Ore, but when he came they could see nothing of it. The peasants said that all was well and that this prognosticated a storm, or a great quantity of fish. Gummer's Ore, however," adds Pontoppidan, " is nothing else than the Kraken, keeping himself always about that spot, and often rising up amongst the rocks and cliffs."[1]

The dimensions of the whale have been so much exaggerated that their size soon became fabulous. St. Brandanus is said to have landed one day upon an island where he and his companions lit a fire and began to cook food. Suddenly the island began to move and they had just time to regain their ships. What they had taken for an island was only a gigantic whale.

The following story is interesting : During the reign of Philip II of Spain, a gigantic whale or sea-monster appeared in the ocean which greatly differed from all the others hitherto seen. Standing half in the water and half above it it had two gigantic fins and sailed along like a ship. A ship

caught sight of the monster, fired and broke one of
its fins. With a terrible noise and howling aloud
the monster turned right into the Straits of Gibraltar
and fell dead on the shore of Valencia. Its mouth
was so large that seven men could stand in it quite
comfortably and a rider on horseback could quite
easily enter it. The corpses of two men were found
in its stomach.[1]

In 1615 one of these sea-monsters came swimming
into the Elbe, while in 1638 a fisherman who tried
to throw a harpoon into such a monster was killed
by an electric shock emanating from the monster.

Numerous folk-tales are found in the Talmud
concerning sea-monsters. The Leviathan is said to
be of an enormous size. " One day," runs one folk-
tale, " we were sailing in a ship and saw a fish which
put its head out of the water, upon which the following words were written : ' I am one of the meanest
creatures that inhabit the sea. I am three hundred
miles in length, and I enter this day into the jaws of
the Leviathan. ' "[2] When the Leviathan is hungry he
sends forth from his mouth a heat so that all the
waters of the deep begin to boil. He dwells in the
Mediterranean Sea, and the waters of the Jordan
fall into his mouth.

Among the many stories relating his adventures
on the sea, Rabbi bar bar Hanah tells the following :

---

[1] See Landrin, *Les monstres marins*, pp. 154–155.
[2] *Baba Bathra*, 74a.

" Once, while on a ship, we came to a gigantic fish at rest, which we supposed to be an island, made a fire and cooked our meal. But when the fish felt the heat, he rolled over, and had not the ship been near, we would certainly have been drowned."[1]

The following folk-tale of the Leviathan is found in the *Alphabetum Siracidis*.

Once upon a time there lived a man who daily instructed his son to put into practice the injunction of the Preacher who said : " Cast thy bread upon the waters, for thou wilt find it after many days."[2] Now it happened that the old man died. The son, remembering his father's teaching, broke his bread and every day threw a piece into the sea. And every day a fish came up, ate the bread and grew so big that he grew stronger and more powerful than all the other fishes whom he oppressed. In their distress the fishes foregathered and decided to bring their complaint before Leviathan, the king of the waters.

" Lord," said the fishes, " there is a big fish dwelling in these waters who has grown so big and strong that we are unable to resist him and we have no power against him. He is so strong that he swallows up every day about twenty or more of us. We are doomed to destruction."

Thus spoke the fishes and implored Leviathan's

---

[1] *Baba Bathra*, 73b.
[2] Eccles. xi. 1.

help. Thereupon Leviathan sent a messenger and summoned the big fish into his presence. The big fish, however, swallowed up the messenger. Leviathan sent up a second messenger who met with a similar fate. When Leviathan saw that the big fish, defying his authority, refused to appear in his presence, he betook himself to the big fish and thus addressed him :

" How is it that among the many fishes dwelling in these waters thou alone hast grown so big and mighty that thou canst swallow up so many of them—none of them being able to resist thee ? "

Thereupon the big fish made answer : " If I have grown so big and strong it is due to the deed of a man dwelling on land. This man brings every day a piece of bread which I consume. Thanks to this daily food, I have grown so strong and big. I consume every morning twenty fishes and every evening thirty."

" And why dost thou eat up thy equals ? " queried Leviathan.

" Because they dare come near me and thus expose themselves to danger. It is their own fault."

Thereupon Leviathan commanded the fish to bring the man, who gave him his daily portion of bread, into his presence.

" To-morrow, my Lord," said the big fish, " I will bring the man into thy presence."

Thereupon he swum to the place on the shore

which the lad was in the habit of visiting daily and where he threw his bread into the water. The fish dug a hole on the shore and when the lad, as was his habit, came up he fell into the water. Immediately the fish who was near, holding his mouth open, swallowed him up and swum back to Leviathan.

" I have brought the man to you, my Lord," he said.

" Spit him out," commanded Leviathan, and the fish obeyed. He spat out the lad whom he had swallowed, and the latter fell into the open mouth of Leviathan.

" My son," said the king of the fishes, " why hast thou thrown thy bread into the water ? "

" I did it," replied the lad, " in obedience to the instruction I have received from my father."

Thereupon Leviathan kissed the lad who had thus honoured the memory of his father and been faithful to the latter's teaching. He taught him the seventy languages spoken in the world and then spat him out upon the land at a distance of three hundred miles from the shore. The lad found himself in a place where the foot of man had yet never trodden. As he was lying on the ground, weary and exhausted, he saw two ravens flying above and he heard them holding converse among themselves. As Leviathan had taught him not only the speech of man but also that of the beasts and the birds, he could understand the language of the ravens too.

"Father," said the younger raven, "look down upon the man lying on the ground; do you think he is dead or alive?"

"I know it not, my son," replied the old raven.

"I will swoop down," said the young raven, "and tear out his eyes, for I have a great desire to eat human eyes." But the raven-father warned his son, saying: "Do not swoop down, my child, for the man may still be alive."

The impetuous young raven, however, disobeyed the prudent advice of his father and swooped down in his eagerness to eat the eyes of the man. The lad was ready for his enemy, and as soon as the bird of prey perched on his forehead he caught hold of its feet and held it fast.

"Father, father," cried the young raven in his distress, "I have fallen into the hands of the man and am kept a prisoner; save me!"

When the raven-father heard his son's cry, he began to weep aloud, crying: "Woe unto my son!" Turning to the lad, he thereupon thus addressed him:

"I wish thou didst understand my speech. If thou dost then listen to my words: get up and dig in the ground whereupon thou art lying; there thou wilt find the treasure of Solomon, King of Israel."

When the lad heard these words which he well

understood, he let the young raven loose and began
to dig the ground where he had been lying. He
found the treasure of King Solomon, which consisted of pearls and precious gems. And the lad
had thus grown rich because Leviathan had taught
him the speech of all the beasts and the birds, and
because he had faithfully carried out his father's
instructions.[1]

One of the many superstitions of sailors with
regard to small fishes is that connected with the
barnacle, a kind of shellfish. For a long time the
belief was current among seafaring people that
when the barnacle adhering to the bottom of the
ship is broken off it becomes a species of a goose.
" I saw the feathers of these barnacles hang out of
the shell at least two inches."

In 1597, the author of the *Herball* wrote as follows :
" There is a small island in Lancashire called the
Pile of Foulders, wherein are found the broken
pieces of old and bruised ships, some whereof have
been cast thither by shipwracke ; and also the
trunks and bodies, with the branches of old rotten
trees cast up there likewise ; whereon is found a
certain spume, or froth, that in time breedeth unto
certaine shels, in shape like those of the muskle,
but sharper pointed and of a whitish colour, wherein
is contained a thing in forme like a lace of silke,
finely woven as it were together, of a whitish colour ;

[1] *Alphabetum Siracidis*, Sect. VII, pp. 5a–6b.

one ende whereof is fastened unto the inside of the shell, even as the fish of oisters and muskles are ; the other ende is made fast under the belly of a rude masse or lumpe, which in time cometh to the shape and forme of a bird. When it is perfectly formed, the shell gapeth open and the first thing that appeareth is the aforesaid lace or string ; next come the legs of a bird hanging out, and as it groweth greater it openeth the shell by degrees, till at length it is all come forth, and hangeth only by the bill ; in a short time after it cometh to full maturity, and falleth into the sea, where it gathers feathers and grows to a fowl bigger than a mallard, and less than a goose, having black legs, and bill or beak, and feathers black and white, spotted in such a manner as is our magpie, called in some places a pie-annet, which the people in Lancashire call by no other name than a tree-goose ; which place, and all those parts adjoining, do so much abound therewith that one of the best may be bought for threepence."[1]

[1] Gerard, *The Herball ;* see also J. E. Harting, *The Ornithology of Shakespeare*, 1871, pp. 249-251.

PHANTOM SHIPS AND APPARITIONS

THE PHANTOM SHIP

In Mather's Magnalia Christi,
　Of the old colonial time,
May be found in prose and legend
　That is here set down in rhyme.

A ship sailed from New Haven,
　And the keen and frosty airs,
That filled her sails at parting,
　Were heavy with good men's prayers.

" O Lord ! if it be thy pleasure,"
　Thus prayed the old divine—
" To bury our friends in the ocean,
　Take them, for they are thine ! "

But Master Lamberton muttered,
　And under his breath, said he,
" This ship is so crank and walty,
　I fear our grave she will be ! "

And the ships that came from England,
　When the winter months were gone,
Brought no tidings of this vessel,
　Nor of Master Lamberton.

This put the people to praying
　That the Lord would let them hear
What in his greater wisdom
　He had done with friends so dear.

And at last their prayers were answered :—
　It was in the month of June,
An hour before the sunset
　Of a windy afternoon,

When, steadily steering landward,
　A ship was seen below,
And they knew it was Lamberton, Master,
　Who sailed so long ago.

On she came, with a cloud of canvas,
　Right against the wind that blew,
Until the eye could distinguish
　The faces of the crew.

Then fell her straining topmasts,
　Hanging tangled in the shrouds,
And her sails were loosened and lifted,
　And blown away like clouds.

And the masts, with all their rigging,
　Fell slowly, one by one,
And the hulk dilated and vanished,
　As a sea-mist in the sun !

And the people who saw this marvel
　Each said unto his friend,
That this was the mould of their vessel,
　And thus her tragic end.

And the pastor of the village
　Gave thanks to God in prayer,
That, to quiet their troubled spirits,
　He had sent this Ship of Air.　　　LONGFELLOW.

CHAPTER X

PHANTOM SHIPS AND APPARITIONS

Seamen an odd compound of exalted feeling and superstition—
Reginald Scott on superstitions of seamen—Phantom ships—
The *Concordia*—" Le vaisseau phantome "—*La Belle Rosalie*
—François the fisherman's boy—Maria Batiste—The Flying
Dutchman—The Wandering Jew—Al Samiri who fashioned
the golden calf—The castle of Falkenberg—The fratricide—
The mysterious boat—The two attendants—The ship sailing
for six hundred years—Playing for the Fratricide's soul—Le
Voltigeur Hollandais—The Voltigeur visits passing ships—
Log entries—Description of the Flying Dutchman—Bernard
Fokke, the Flying Dutchman—The captain who had sold
his soul to the devil—Spectre ships on the Cornish coast—
The souls of shipwrecked mariners—Captain Marryat's
Flying Dutchman—Wagner's *Fliegende Holläender*—Giant
ships—The *Refanu*—Gargantua—Superstitions in Finistère—
The giant ship *Mannigfual*—The island of Bornholm—Devil
ships—The saint and the devil—The burning cask of tar—
" Forward, in the name of Jesus "—The Bay of the Departed—
Ghosts and apparitions—The ghost of the murdered bride—
Jean Moyatos, the Greek sailor—The figure in white—The
cook with a short leg—A story told by Sir Walter Scott—Bill
Jones and the irascible captain—" Bill is with me now "—
The seamen who smelt a ghost—A dead rat.

IT has been rightly said that sailors are one
of the oddest compounds in existence, having
habits and feelings and even a language peculiar
to themselves. Noble virtues and exalted feelings
mix and mingle in seafaring men with gross habits
and degrading vices. Heroes in an hour of danger,
sailors are often mere children in sympathetic
feeling. Amidst the blood and slaughter of battle

they are dauntless in their defiance of death, and yet the sight of a coffin on shore will make them shrink with apprehension.

" Innumerable," wrote Reginald Scott,[1] " are the reports of accidents unto those who frequent the sea, such as fishermen and sailors, who discuss the noises, flashes, shadows, echoes, and other visible appearances, nightly seen and heard upon the water."

Apparitions and ghosts are still firmly believed in by sailors and are a source of terror to them. Many tales attesting the belief of sailors in ghosts and apparitions are related by Sir Walter Scott (*Demonology and Witchcraft*), and in the *New Catalogue of Vulgar Errors*.[2]

PHANTOM SHIPS

Numerous are the tales current among sailors of phantom ships. These tales are no doubt the result of poetical illusion, but to the sailor, who has witnessed scenes of terror and uncanny sights the landsman can never dream of, they are the sober truth. The sailor often sees unearthly visions and hears unearthly voices and, more than the landsman, he clings to his belief in the supernatural. Thousands of landsmen believe in the possibility of seeing ghosts, and psychical research societies

[1] *Discovery of Witchcraft.*
[2] See Hazlitt, *Dictionary of Faiths and Folklore*, s.v. " Sailors' and Marine Superstitions."

investigate these beliefs and endeavour to explain them scientifically. No wonder that the sailor should still cling to his belief in phantom ships and apparitions.

Some ships are seen only once, while others make their appearance at regular intervals or at certain moments. They foretell either wreck or disaster or convey a warning, thus enabling those who behold them to escape. Some such ships are indicating an approaching storm. When French fishermen at Heyst see a phantom ship called *Concordia*, manned by red-capped trucks, passing along the beach from the great dune of the Renard upon the sands lying between the sea and the dunes, they know that there is danger in store.[1]

Another story of a phantom ship, entitled " Le vaisseau phantome," is related in the *Revue des Traditions populaires*.[2] Its contents are briefly as follows :

Three ships were to sail from Dieppe, the quaint fishing town, for the western fisheries. One of these, *La Belle Rosalie*, was to make her maiden voyage, and François, hitherto a fisherman's boy, was engaged as wheelman. He said good-bye to his sweetheart Maria Batiste, whom he was going to lead to the altar when *La Belle Rosalie* returned. In the early morning all Dieppe came to witness the

---

[1] See *Revue des Trad. pop.*, XV, p. 9 ; XVII, p. 472.
[2] See Vol. VI, p. 416 ; A. Bosquet, *La Normandie pittoresque*.

departure of *La Belle Rosalie*. There were proud
fathers and weeping mothers and sisters, and
fiancées bidding a tremulous farewell to their lovers.
Maria Batiste was among the latter, and François
standing at the wheel could see her at the pier
among the throng waving her hand. Out into the
sunlit sea glided *La Belle Rosalie*.

Months passed and summer drifted, but no
word came from the vessel. Some ships have come
back buffeted by the seas, but many others have
been wrecked by storms, many lives have been lost,
and many homes are saddened. For the departed
sailors the mothers or wives burn tapers, and bells
are tolled and prayers are recited for their souls.
No bells, however, are tolled, no prayers recited,
and no tapers burned for the men who went out to
sea on the *Belle Rosalie*.

Poor Maria Batiste wandered day by day along the
white cliffs, but in vain did she strain her eyes across
the misty channel in the hope of perceiving on the
horizon *La Belle Rosalie* and François her swain.
In vain did she question sailors and mates, but no
news had come of *La Belle Rosalie*. The vessel
was missing, that was all they knew. Summer
passed, and the dreary month of November with
its falling leaves and moaning storms came. The
Day of the Dead came, which is on the second day
of that month. Prayers are recited for the repose
of the souls of the dead.

THE PHANTOM SHIP

Flemish engraving (between 1480 and 1490

Maria Batiste went out at dawn with her sister, in the hope of meeting her affianced. She was looking out upon the water, when suddenly the sorrowing and waiting bride, pointing her finger to the sea, cried : " There is *La Belle Rosalie*, she is coming, sister ! There is François, my François, standing at the wheel, as I saw him last, but how pale he is." Suddenly the rush of dawn came, the mist rolled back silently and the phantom ship, *La Belle Rosalie*, faded into space.

Another story of a phantom ship is told by Gregor in *Folklore of the North Coast of Scotland*. It is a big ship which was lost with all on board and from time to time makes its appearance with a ghostly crew. It is considered as an omen of disaster.

" THE FLYING DUTCHMAN "

The story of *The Flying Dutchman* is well known. It is a story, due to the imagination of sailors, of a hardy and fearless seaman condemned to wander eternally on the surface of the waters. It has rightly been pointed out that the legends of deathless punishment at sea have their counterparts on shore in those of the Wandering Jew, Cartaphilus, or in that of Al Samiri, the maker of the golden calf. The story of the Wandering Jew is too well known to require repetition, but a few words may be devoted to the legend of Al Samiri.

It was a man named Al Samiri who, understanding the founder's art, cast all the golden rings and bracelets which the Israelites had borrowed from the Egyptians into a furnace, to melt them into one mass. When the gold was melted, Samiri threw in a handful of sand which he had taken from under the hoof of Gabriel's horse. A calf came out and bellowed like a living one, born of a cow. When Moses came down from heaven and saw what had happened and was told by Aaron that Samiri had fashioned the golden calf which the Israelites had worshipped, he would have slain Samiri, but the Lord commanded him to spare his life, place him under ban and send him away. Like a wild beast Samiri is wandering ever since from one end of the earth to the other. Men shun and avoid him, and he himself, whenever he comes near men, exclaims : " Touch me not."[1]

The earliest story of a seaman condemned to wander and which has given rise to the legends of *The Flying Dutchman* type runs as follows :

At the old castle of Falkenberg, in the province of Limburg, a spectre walks at night, and a voice from the ruins is heard to cry : " Murder ! Murder ! " And it cries toward the north, and the south, and the east, and the west, and before the cries there go two small flames, which accompany him whitherso-

---

[1] Weil, *Biblische Legenden der Muselmaenner*, p. 172 ; Rappoport, *Myths and Legends of Israel*, Vol. II, pp. 383-384.

ever he turns. And the voice has cried for six hundred years, and so long also have the two flames wandered.

Six hundred years ago the beautiful castle stood in its full glory, and was inhabited by two brothers of the noble race of Falkenberg. Their names were Waleran and Reginald, and they both loved Alexia, the daughter of the Count of Cleves. Waleran, favoured by the Count and his wife, having gained the bride, Reginald vowed vengeance, and having concealed himself in the nuptial chamber, slew his brother and his bride. In his dying struggles, however, Waleran imprinted on the fratricide's face the form of his bloody hand.

Now there dwelt a holy hermit in the forest to whom the conscience-stricken murderer went for consolation. He confessed his sin and showed his face with the print of the bloody hand. Of so foul a deed the hermit dared not to absolve him, but he told him, after a night's vigil, that he must journey toward the north until he should find no more land, and then a sign would be given him. Thus the fratricide started on his wandering journey, accompanied by a white form on the right hand and a black form on the left.

He thus journeyed for many a day, and many a week, and many a month, until one morning he found no more earth beneath his feet and saw the wide ocean before him. At the same moment a boat approached the shore, and a man that was in it made a sign to him and said : " We expected thee." Then the fratricide knew that this was the sign, and he stepped into the boat still attended by the two forms, and they rowed to a large ship with all the sails set, and when they were in the ship the boatmen disappeared and the ship sailed away.

The fratricide, with his two attendants, descended into a room below where stood a table and chairs. Each of the two forms then took a seat at the table, and the black one drew forth a pair of dice and began to play for the soul of Reginald. Six hundred years has that ship now been sailing without either helm or helmsman, and so long have the two forms been playing for Reginald's soul. Their game will last until the last day. Mariners sailing in the North Sea say that they often meet with the infernal vessel.[1]

Jal,[2] describes the belief of sailors in *The Flying Dutchman* as follows :

There was once a hardy and reckless sea-captain who believed neither in God, nor saints, nor anything else. He was a Dutchman. One day he sailed to go south—and all went well as far as the latitude of the Cape of Good Hope. Here, however, a storm arose and the ship being in great danger, the crew and passengers advised the captain to put in

---

[1] Thorpe, *Northern Mythology*, Vol. II.
[2] *Scènes de la vie maritime*, Vol. I.

shore. But the latter only laughed at the fears of his crew and passengers. He sang terrible songs and scoffed and laughed at the tempest and blasphemed Providence.

Suddenly a cloud opened and a huge celestial figure descended upon the deck of the ship. Crew and passengers were seized with terror, but the captain continued to smoke his pipe and did not even raise his cap when the celestial figure addressed him.

" You are mad, captain," said the figure, to which the captain replied : " And you are an uncivil fellow ; I don't ask anything from you, and if you don't get out, at once, I will blow your brains out."

Thereupon the godless captain seized one of his pistols, cocked it and fired at the cloud-figure. The shot, of course, instead of hitting the celestial cloud-form, pierced the captain's hand. Enraged, the rascal jumped up to hit the cloud-form a blow in the face, but behold ! his arm dropped by his side paralysed with palsy. Then the celestial figure which had descended from the clouds said :

" You are accursed, captain, and Heaven sentences you to sail for ever without ever being able to put into port or harbour. You shall have neither beer nor tobacco, but shall drink gall at all times and chew redhot iron for your quid. You shall watch eternally, and you shall never sleep when sleepy, for as soon as you will close your eyes a long sword will pierce your body. Since it was your pleasure to torment sailors you shall continue to do so, for you shall be the evil one of the sea. Ceaselessly you shall wander throughout all latitudes and have neither rest nor fine weather. The sight of your ship which shall hover about to the end of time will bring misfortune to those who see it."

Thus spoke the celestial figure, but the captain only replied : " I defy you ! " The cloud-figure disappeared and with it the crew and passengers, and the captain found himself alone on the deck with only the ship's boy by his side.

The Flying Dutchman or the *Voltigeur* has been sailing since in heavy weather and his whole pleasure is doing harm to poor sailors. It is the *Voltigeur* who sends white squalls, who wrecks ships or leads them on false courses.

There are seamen who say that the *Voltigeur* or *Flying Dutchman* has the audacity to visit passing ships. Often he sends letters on board ships he meets, and if the captain reads them he is lost ; he becomes a madman and his ship dances in the air, turns over while pitching violently. The *Flying Dutchman* paints himself as he will, changing six times a day, so as not to be recognized. Sometimes he has the appearance of a heavy Dutch vessel, hardly able to bluff his heavy quarters into the wind, while at other times he becomes a light corsair

scouring the sea. His crew are accursed as well
as he, for it is a gang of hardened sinners.

Such was the tale of *The Flying Dutchman* as told
by French sailors of the eighteenth century.

English and American sailors tell stories of *The
Flying Dutchman*, and the diaries of English sailors
and log entries made as late as 1835 and 1881
contain references to *The Flying Dutchman*:

" We had been in dirty weather, as the sailors say,
for several days, and to begin the afternoon I
commanded after-dinner narratives to the French
officers and passengers about *The Flying Dutchman*.
The wind which had been freshening during the
evening now blew a stiff gale, and we proceeded
on deck. Dark and heavy clouds coursed with
rapidity across the bright moon, whose lustre is
so peculiar in the southern hemisphere, and we
could see a distance off from eight to ten miles on
the horizon.

" Suddenly the second officer, a fine Marseilles
sailor who had been among the foremost in the
cabin in laughing at and ridiculing the story of the
Flying Dutchman, ascended the weather rigging,
and exclaimed : " Voilà la volant Hollandais ! "
The captain sent for his night-glass and soon observed : " It is very strange, but there is a ship
bearing down on us with *all sail set*, while we
dare scarcely show a pocket-handkerchief to the
breeze.

" In a few minutes the stranger was visible to all on deck, her rig plainly discernible, and people on her poop ; she seemed to near us with the rapidity of lightning, and apparently wished to pass under our quarter for the purpose of speaking. The captain, a resolute Bordeaux mariner, said it was quite incomprehensible and sent for the trumpet to hail an answer, when in an instant, and while we were all on the *qui vive*, the stranger totally disappeared, and was seen no more."[1]

Another entry was made in 1881 in the *Bacchante*. It runs as follows: "At four a.m. *The Flying Dutchman* crossed our bows. A strange, red light, as of a phantom ship all aglow, in the midst of which light the masts, spars and sails of a brig two hundred yards distant stood out in strong relief as she came up. The look-out man on the forecastle reported her as close on the port bow, where also the officer of the watch from the bridge clearly saw her, as did also the quarter-deck midshipman, who was sent forward at once to the forecastle ; but on arriving there no vestige nor any sign whatever of any material ship was to be seen either near or right away to the horizon, the night being clear and the sea calm. Thirteen persons altogether saw her, but whether it was van Diemen or *The Flying Dutchman*, or who, she must remain unknown.

---

[1] English log entry made in 1835 by R. M. Martin, quoted by W. Bassett, *Wanderships*, p. 57.

The *Tourmaline* and *Cleopatra*, who were sailing on our starboard bow, flashed to ask whether we had seen the strange red light.[1]

German sailors, too, tell many stories of such ships condemned to wander eternally over the surface of the waters. There is one story according to which the unhappy captain had made a contract with the Devil. The captain and three of his men, aged men with long white beards, are still seen by Indians. When they are hailed, the ship disappears. The appearance of *The Flying Dutchman* is described elsewhere as follows: " She was painted yellow, of yellow were the dim churchyard lines that I marked her hull was coated with. She was low in the bows with a great spring aft, crowned by a kind of double poop, one above another, and what I could see of the stern was almost pear-shape, supposing the fruit inverted with the stalk sliced off. She had three masts each with a large protected circular top, resembling turrets, sails of the texture of cobwebs hung from her squareyards."[2]

According to one legend Bernard Fokke is *The Flying Dutchman*. He was a mariner who lived in the seventeeth century, a daring and clever sailor who could make the voyage from Batavia to Holland in ninety days. Such fast journeys were supposed to be due to the help of the Devil and to the magic

[1] *Ibid.*, p. 56.
[2] Quoted by Bassett, l.c., pp. 59–60.

powers of Fokke. This belief found the more
easily credence since Fokke was a powerfully built
man, very strong, ugly and of a violent temper.
One day he did not return from his sea-voyage,
and people said that the Devil had claimed his own.
For the many sins he had committed Fokke was
said to have been condemned to wander eternally
with his ship between the Cape of Good Hope and
the southern extremity of America. All the mariners
in the Indian Ocean pretended to have seen the
vessel. The captain and the crew, consisting of
three sailors, were old men with long beards. As
soon as someone tried to address them the vessel
immediately disappeared. The phantom ship was
usually seen at night, but sometimes also during the
day. One day a few daring sailors went out in a
barque and tried to board it, but when they thought
they had touched it, the phantom ship vanished.[1]

On the Cornish coast spectre ships are supposed
to be seen before wrecks ; they are generally
shrouded in mist ; but the crew of one was said to
consist of two men, a woman and a dog. These
ships vanish at some well-known point. Jack
Harry's lights, too, herald a storm ; they are so
called from the man who first saw them. These
appear on a phantom vessel resembling the one that
will be lost.[2]

[1] *Ausland*, 1841, No. 237.
[2] *Folklore Journal*, 1887, p. 189.

Fishermen in Normandy firmly believed, and a good many of them still cling to this belief, that when the prayers for the souls of shipwrecked mariners are not efficacious, a phantom ship appears. A tempest suddenly arises and a ship is seen at sea, struggling with winds and waves. Then suddenly the vessel is driven with lightning rapidity towards the port, and on entering, the horrified spectators on the quay recognize in the ship those who had been reported lost at sea years before. Assistance is given to bring the ship into a safe place, ropes are thrown on board, which are caught by the crew, and the vessel is attached to the quay. The news spreads, and widows and children and friends of the seamen supposed to have been drowned rush to the spot. Cries of recognition arise. " There is my father, husband, brother, or lover." No answer, however, is heard from the vessel, not one cry from the crew, although the figures can clearly be seen. Not a lip moves, nor is any sign of recognition heard. At length the bells sound the hour of midnight, and a fog steals over the sea. On clearing off after a few moments the vessel has suddenly disappeared, to the great distress of the spectators.[1]

The phantom ship or *The Flying Dutchman* is the subject of many literary works. Captain Marryat's *The Phantom Ship* and Wagner's Opera

[1] See Jones, *Credulities*, pp. 83–84.

Der Fliegende Holländer are well known. There
is a short poem entitled : " The Phantom Ship," by
Longfellow in his *Birds of Passage*. This poem, as
Longfellow explains, is based on the story related
by Cotton Mather in his work *Magnalia Christi*.[1]

GIANT SHIPS

Stories of and beliefs in giant ships are also
current among seamen of all nations. Thus in the
stories of the sea and in the mythologies of all
nations are to be found tales of ships of vast dimensions. Such is the *Refanu* of Swedish story, which is
so vast that a journey from poop to prow lasts
three weeks and the orders are transmitted on horseback. It has an inn in every block.[2]

In the popular traditions about Gargantua it is
said that he built a giant boat for whose timbers he
felled a whole forest.[3] There is a story current in
the French province of Var of a giant ship named
La Patte Luzerne, which used to haunt the coast of
Provence. The masts were so high that the cabin-
boys who went aloft to the tops came down on the
other side grey-bearded old men.[4] Such giant ships
are also *La Grande Chasse Foudre*, described by
French sailors,[5] and the *Merry Dun* of Dover, and
the Frisian ship *Manningfual*.[6]

[1] See also Mélusine, Vol. II.   [2] *Germania*, 33, p. 109.
[3] See Sébillot, *Gargantua*, p. 18.
[4] See *Rev. des Trad. pop.*, XII, p. 30.   [5] See Jal.
[6] See Thorpe, l.c., III, p. 28.

Old sailors in the Finistère tell stories of foundered ships returned to haunt the coast with their ghostly crews. These ships expand extraordinarily. One old sailor related that he had been one of the crew of a brig that was wrecked. He was the only survivor, and he often met his ship on distant seas afterwards and each time she was larger than before. In many localities in Lower Brittany there are stories current of a huge ship manned by giant human forms. Orders on this strange vessel are transmitted through huge conch-shells, and as the noise is heard at a distance of miles it is easy to avoid this craft, for if it should be allowed to come near any vessel its crew, it is said, would suddenly disappear.[1]

Thorpe relates of the giant ship *Mannigfual*. This ship is so vast that the captain always rides about the deck on horseback, for the purpose of giving his orders. The sailors who climb up the rigging when young come down again stricken in years with grey beards and hair. While so employed they keep themselves alive by frequent visits to the blocks of the cordage, which contain rooms for refection.

This monstrous vessel once steered its course from the Atlantic Ocean into the English Channel; but being unable on account of the narrowness of the strait to pass between Dover and Calais, the

---

[1] See Mélusine, Sept. 1884.

captain had the lucky thought of having the whole
starboard side smeared over with white soap. This
operation proved effectual and the *Mannigfual*
passed through safely and entered the North Sea.
From that time the cliffs of Dover got their white
soapy appearance, from the soap that was rubbed
off, and the foam raised by the motion of the vessel.

Once the giant ship found itself in the Baltic,
but the crew soon discovered that the water was too
shallow. To get afloat again, they found it necessary
to throw the ballast, together with the dirt and ashes
of the galley, overboard. From the ballast the isle
of Bornholm derives its origin and from the rubbish
the little neighbouring isle of Christiansö.

DEVIL-SHIPS

Sailors also tell stories of devil-ships, and the
tales current among them are numerous. The early
mariners, unacquainted with currents, were naturally
struck by the sight of a ship moving against a light
breeze, and the freaks of wind and wave for which
they had no explanation gave rise to and inspired
such beliefs. The superstitious belief existed for
ages and still lurks in the corners of the mind of
simple seafaring folk. Demons and evil spirits
caused storms and wind, and ships were said to be
possessed or enchanted or driven by the Devil and
his assistants. The belief in the demons of the

sea is even now strong among sailors and many of them will hesitate to rescue a drowning man for fear of angering those demons of the sea.[1]

There is an incident in Sir Walter Scott's novel, *The Pirate*, illustrating this superstition. Bryce the pedlar refuses to help Mordaunt to save the ship-wrecked sailor from drowning, and he even remonstrates with him on the rashness of such a deed. " Are you mad ? " says the pedlar ; " you that have lived so long in Zetland, to risk the saving of a drowning man ? Wot ye not, if you bring him to life again, he will be sure to do you some capital injury ? " A similar superstition exists among the Kilda Islanders and the boatmen of the Danube, among English and French sailors. It exists among the Hindus and the Kamtchadals. The former do not save a man from drowning in the sacred Ganges, while the latter say that he who delivers a man from drowning will be drowned himself.[2]

The Kamtchadals even went further. They believed that if a man fell into the water it was a great sin for himself to get out, for as he had been destined to be drowned he did wrong in not drowning, wherefore no one should let him into his dwelling, nor speak to him nor give him food or a wife, but he should be reckoned for dead. When a man fell into the water while others were standing by,

---

[1] See Gregor, l.c.
[2] See Bastian, *Der Mensch*, Vol. III, p. 210 ; Krachennikov, *Voyage en Sibérie*, Vol. III, p. 72.

instead of helping him out, they should drown him by force.[1]

The superstition is also found in Bohemia where fishermen, about seventy years ago, were still afraid of venturing to save a drowning man from the waters, lest the demon of the sea take away their luck in fishing and drown themselves at the first opportunity.[2]   The reason of this widespread superstition is explained by Tylor as the reluctance to deprive the water-spirits and demons of their victims. Once the sea-demons or spirits claim a victim, it would be a rash defiance of deity or a powerful spirit to rescue the drowning man. The water-demon was sure to wreak his vengeance on those who dared to interfere with him.[3]

The Fire of St. Elmo is connected with a devil-ship. One day, a French legend relates, Satan built a huge ship on which he gathered many lost souls. With his craft, which smelled of sulphur and sowed a pest for a hundred miles about her, Satan committed many piracies and rejoiced at his exploits, making merry when new souls were brought upon deck. In the end the exploits of Satan enraged Saint Elmo. On one dark night he stealthily approached the devil-ship and pierced her hull. Satan himself had just time to save himself by

[1] See Steller, *Kamtschatka*, pp. 265, 274.
[2] See J. V. Grohmann, *Aberglauben und Gebräuche in Boehmen*, p. 12.
[3] See E. B. Tylor, *Primitive Culture*, Vol. I, pp. 109-110.

swimming. And henceforth, on dark nights, when the air is warm, the ship burns again and the flames mount to the sky and the sulphur can be smelled for miles.[1]

The Devil, Pomeranian sailors believe, is sailing the seas in a burning cask of tar. These self-impelled ships are said either to have been built by the Devil himself or by human hands, and to have fallen into the power of devils and evil spirits who are constantly waging war against mankind. Such is the tale of Icelandic fishermen :

The moaning is the language of vessels, but not everybody can understand the speech of the ships. One day a man heard two vessels beached upon the sand conversing with each other.

" We shall never be together again," said the first vessel, " because to-morrow, in spite of the bad weather, my master will put to sea."

" I will not go," said the other vessel, " unless the Devil himself had a hand in it."

On the following morning the master came and in spite of the menacing weather he ordered the crew to launch the craft.

" Forward, au nom de Jésu," he called.

The vessel would not move, and all the efforts of the crew proved futile.

" Forward, then," cried the angry master, " au nom du diable."

[1] See Mélusine, 1884, Aug.

Immediately the vessel slid into the water, floated away, but never since have either craft or crew been heard of.[1]

One of the superstitions current among seafaring people relating to phantom ships and apparitions is that about the Bay of the Departed in Brittany. It is told by Sir Walter Scott in his *Count Robert of Paris*, after Procopius.

Beyond Gaul and nearly opposite to it, but separated by an arm of the sea, lies a ghastly region on which clouds and tempests for ever rest, and which is known to its Continental neighbours as the abode to which departed spirits are sent after this life. On one side of the strait dwell a few fishermen, men possessed of a strange character, and enjoying singular privileges in consideration of thus being the living ferrymen who, performing the office of the heathen Charon, carry the spirits of the departed to the island which is their residence after death. At the dead of the night these fishermen are in rotation summoned to perform the duty by which they seem to hold permission to reside on this strange coast. A knock is heard at the door of his cottage, who holds the turn of this singular office, founded by no mortal hand; a whispering as of a decaying breeze summons the ferryman to his duty. He hastens to his work on the seashore, and has no sooner launched it than he perceives its hull sink

---

[1] Sébillot, *Le Folklore des Pêcheurs*, p. 367.

sensibly in the water, so as to express the weight of the dead with whom it is filled. No form is seen ; and though voices are heard, yet the accents are undistinguishable, as of one who speaks in his sleep.[1]

The place whence the boat with its ghostly freight was supposed to put off was near Raz, near the Bay of Souls, in the extreme west of Finistère. It is opposite the island of Slint where nightly the skeletons of drowned mariners are said to dance. Here are also the abyss of Plogoff and the wild moors studded with Druid monuments.

To be distinguished from phantom and spectre-ships are the spectres and apparitions which have such a strong hold on the minds of sailors. Their naturally superstitious minds and feelings and their effect on a nervous temperament result in their often conjuring up an apparition and maintaining that they had seen it with their own eyes.

Numerous are the ghost stories related by mariners, and in modern times seamen are mostly inclined to believe in ghosts and apparitions.

In the year 1530 Count Otto Heinrich sailed to the Holy Land. On his return journey he crossed a ship whence came a loud warning shout :

" Out of the way, out of the way ; Stout Enderle of Ketch is coming."

[1] See also Jones, l.c., p. 82 ; Tylor, *Primitive Culture ;* Gould, S. B., *Curious Myths*, p. 530–531.

The Count and his chamberlain Muecken-
haeuser knew well the godless village mayor of
Ketch and were greatly surprised. When they
reached home they made enquiries and found that
the day and hour of Enderle's death coincided
exactly with the time when they had met the ship
and heard the mysterious shout.[1]

In a Scottish legend a sailor is said to have suddenly seen the ghost of his murdered bride. She
appeared in the shape of a brilliant light over the
water. The nearer she came the more distinctly appeared the human shape. At last she called him
by name, and both seaman and bride disappeared
in the brilliant light. The dead bride had come to
claim her affianced from the living.

Another girl had died on the scaffold and she
came to claim her lover in the open sea. He had
pledged his word to be faithful to her in life or death.
A storm broke out, and the ghost of the girl,
accompanied by a gigantic phantom, appeared.
The gale raged until she had seized the sailor and
vanished with him, when the storm abated.[2]

Another ghost story at sea is told by Grant in
his *Mysteries* :

Five days after the barque *Pontiac* of Liverpool
left Callao, Jean Moyatos, a Greek sailor, murdered
one of his fellow-seamen and stabbed another in
such a dangerous manner that his life was despaired

---

[1] Heims, *Seespuk*.　　[2] See Heims, l.c., p. 125.

of. The murder occurred under the following circumstances. Two nights before the fatal occurrence the mate of the *Pontiac* was standing near the man at the helm, no other person being on the quarter-deck at the time, when the latter in great terror called out :

" What is that near the cabin door ? " The mate replied that he saw nothing.

The steersman, however, much terrified, said that the figure he saw was that of a strange-looking man, of ghostly appearance. Almost immediately afterwards he exclaimed :

" There he is again, standing at the cabin window."

The mate saw no figure either at the window or at any other part of the quarter-deck, though he looked round and round. Next day the report went from one to the other part of the deck that a ghost was on board, which filled some of the sailors with alarm, while others made a jest of it. Next night a boy was so dreadfully alarmed in his bunk by something he saw or felt, that he cried out so loudly as to waken all the seamen in bed. The boy was sure that it was the ghost seen the previous night that had frightened him, and others of more mature years were inclined to think so too. More than half of the crew believed that something supernatural was in the ship and that some calamity would soon happen.

There were, however, two sailors on board who did not believe the ghost stories, and these were the man subsequently murdered and his companion who was stabbed. The former joked with the boy about the ghost, and said he would have his knife well-sharpened and ready for the ghost if it appeared next night. He would give it a stab and chuck it overboard. Moyatos overheard what was said as to stabbing and throwing overboard, and as he only imperfectly understood the English language and had also previously supposed that there was a plot against him, he thought that the threats were made against him. As a result he resolved to protect himself.

A few hours after the jesting had taken place, he stabbed the two men who had carried on the jest. The terror of the sailors who believed that there was a ghost on board became overwhelming. The report went round the ship that peculiar noises were heard below, and whether in bed or on watch the seamen had great dread. When the ship lay moored in the docks of Leith, two of the crew who had agreed to sleep on board became so frightened that they refused to remain in the vessel at night.

Jean Moyatos, the Greek sailor, on being brought to trial, was found to be insane.[1]

Another incident, illustrating this superstition

[1] J. Grant, *The Mysteries of All Nations*, pp. 583–585.

of sailors and their belief in apparitions and ghosts, is related in *Blackwood's Magazine* (1840).

Between one and two in the morning, while I was having charge of the middle watch, I was suddenly taken ill and obliged to send for the officer next in turn. Going down on the gun-deck, I sent my boy for a light. In the meanwhile I sat down on a chest in the steerage, under the after-grating. Suddenly I felt a gentle squeeze by a very cold hand. I started and saw a figure in white.

" God's my life," I cried, " who is that ? " The figure stood up and gazed at me for a short time, stooped its head to get a more perfect view, then sighed aloud, repeated three times the exclamation " Oh ! " and instantly vanished.

It was a fine night, although the moon shed but a feeble light so that I could see little of the features. I only noticed a rather tall figure, white-clad. My boy having by this time returned with a light, I sent him down to the cabins of all the officers. He came back and brought word that none of the officers had been stirring. When I came to St. Helena I heard of my sister's death and found the time of her apparition and her demise nearly coinciding.

The following story illustrating the superstitious belief of sailors is told by Brand in his *Popular Antiquities* :

The cook of a vessel belonging to Newcastle-upon-

Tyne had died during the homeward journey. He had one of his legs shorter than the other, which caused a peculiarity of gait when he walked. A few nights after the body had been committed to the deep, the mate alarmed the captain by telling him that the cook was walking before the ship. All the crew came on deck to watch the apparition. The captain came on deck and he really saw something that moved just as the cook had been accustomed to walk. He ordered the ship to be steered towards the object and then it was discovered that the cause of all the terror and panic was part of a maintop, the remains of some wreck, floating before the ship.[1]

In his *Letters on Demonology and Witchcraft*, Sir Walter Scott relates a story showing the superstition of seamen and their belief in and dread of ghosts and apparitions.

A sailor had in his youth become a mate in a slave vessel from Liverpool, of which town he was a native. The captain of the ship was a man of variable temper, sometimes kind and courteous to his men, but sometimes, when he was in a fit of humour, very violent, cruel and tyrannical. Now there was an old sailor on board whose name was Bill Jones, or some such name, to whom the captain had taken a particular dislike. He seldom spoke to this seaman without abuse and threats which,

---

[1] Brand, *Popular Antiquities*.

however, the old seaman with that freedom which
sailors take in merchant vessels, was not slow in
returning.

On one occasion Bill Jones was rather slow, or
appeared to be slow in getting on the yard. The
captain, according to his custom, abused him and
called him a lubberly rascal who left others to do
his duty while he himself was only growing fat.
The seaman was not slow in his reply. He answered
the captain in an impertinent and saucy tone and his
answer almost amounted to mutiny. The captain,
flying into a towering passion, ran down to his cabin
where he fetched a blunderbuss loaded with slugs and
returned on deck. Deliberately taking aim at the
seaman, he fired and mortally wounded him. Bill
Jones was carried down from the yard, and stretched
on the deck, evidently dying.

Fixing his eyes on the captain, he said : " Sir,
you have done for me, *but I will never leave you.*"
The captain, by way of reply, swore at him for a fat
lubber. He threatened to have him thrown into the
slave-kettle where they made food for the negroes,
and see how much fat he had got. The seaman,
that is Bill Jones, died and he was actually thrown
into the slave-kettle.

Now the captain commanded the crew to keep
absolute silence on the subject of what had passed.
The mate, however, was not willing to give an
absolute and explicit promise, and the captain

ordered him to be confined below. A day or two afterwards the captain came down to the mate and asked him whether he intended to deliver him up for trial when the vessel reached home. The mate, who was rather tired of his confinement in that sultry climate, promised his captain to keep silence and obtained his liberty. When he again mingled among the crew he found them impressed with the idea that the ghost of the dead man appeared amongst them when they had a spell of duty, especially if a sail was to be handled, upon which occasion the ghost of Bill Jones was sure to be out upon the yard before any of them.

The narrator of the story maintained that he had seen the apparition frequently. He firmly believed that the captain too saw it, but that he took no notice of it for some time, and the crew, terrified at the violent temper of the man, dared not call his attention to it.

One night the captain invited the mate to his cabin to have a glass of grog with him. He assumed a very grave and anxious aspect at this interview and thus addressed the mate :

" Jack, I need not tell you what sorts of hands we have got on board with us ; *he* told me that he would never leave me, *and he has kept his word.* You only see him now and again, but he is always with *me*, always at my side and never out of sight. I see him at this very moment, and I am determined to bear it no longer. I have resolved to leave you."

The mate replied that his leaving the vessel while out of sight of any land was quite impossible. He therefore suggested that if the captain feared any danger or bad consequences from what had happened he should run for the west of Ireland, or France, and there go ashore and leave him, the mate, to carry the vessel to Liverpool. The captain, however, shook his head gloomily, and repeated his determination to leave the ship. At this moment the mate was called away to the deck, but the instant he got up the companion ladder, he heard a splash. Looking over the ship's side, he saw that the captain had thrown himself into the sea from the quarter gallery, and was swimming astern at the rate of six knots an hour. When he was just about to sink, he made a last exertion, sprang half out of the water, and clasping his hands towards the mate, exclaimed : " Bill is with me now," whereupon he sank, to be seen no more.[1]

Brand tells a good story with reference to the belief of sailors in ghosts. " About half a dozen of the sailors on board a man-of-war took it into their heads that there was a ghost in the ship ; and being asked by the captain what reason they had to apprehend any such thing, they told him they were sure of it, for they *smelt him*. The captain

[1] Sir Walter Scott, *Letters on Demonology and Witchcraft.*

first laughed at them and called them a parcel of lubbers and advised them not to entertain any such silly notions as these, but mind their work. It passed on very well for a day or two ; but one night, being in another ghost-smelling humour, they all came to the captain and told him that they were quite certain there was a ghost, and he was somewhere behind the small beer-barrels. The captain, quite enraged at their folly, was determined they should have something to be frightened at in earnest ; and so ordered the boatswain's mate to give them all a dozen of lashes with a cat-o'-nine-tails, by which means the ship was entirely cleared of ghosts during the remainder of the voyage. However, when the barrels were removed some time after, they found a dead rat, or some such thing, which was concluded by the rest of the crew to be the ghost which had been smelt a little before."[1]

[1] See Hazlitt, W. C., *Faith and Folklore*, Vol. II, p. 530.

OMENS AND CEREMONIES

CHAPTER XI

OMENS AND CEREMONIES

Omens and signs—Miraculous agencies for good or for evil—The
seasons of the year and the days of the week—The encounter
of certain persons—Lawyers and tailors—Priests synonymous
with Jonah—Scottish fishermen never pronounce the words
" kirk " and " minister " at sea—Barefooted women—The
sea grows angry at sight of a woman—Pliny's view—Lame
man a bad omen—Finns and Laplanders—The names of *Ross,
Coull,* and *Whyte*—Hares, pigs and cats—To talk of hares is
an ominous sign—Lucky and unlucky days—Superstitions
about Friday—The days of the week—Saturday and Friday—
The king of Poland who missed favourable winds—Friday
connected with the Crucifixion—The goddess Freya—The
Eternal Feminine—Vessels which did leave on a Friday—Lord
Byron's superstitions—Stolen timber—A fly in a glass—A
child's caul—French and Yiddish proverbs—Unlucky to be
numbered—The loss of a water-bucket or a mop—Superstitions
of American sailors—Old salts on lost ships—Bells and
seamen's superstitions—The cemetery of St. Leven—The
bells of Helgoland and Nijkerk—The Kentsham bell—The
ceremony of christening a ship—Ceremonies in France and
Scotland—Christening of ships in Britanny—Biscuits and
wine—The wood godfather—The launching of vessels in
Scotland—Whisky, bread and cheese—A custom in Japan—
Blessing of ships—The bishop of Bangor—Old boats, unlucky
to break them up—The loss and tearing of a ship's colours.

SAILORS are as a rule very superstitious
and puerile in their apprehensions of omens.
They care as little what becomes of them
as any set of people under the sun, and yet no one
is so apprehensive of omens and signs as are sailors
and fishermen.[1] The omens and prognostics under

[1] See Brand, *Popular Antiquities*, Vol. III, p. 125.

which the ancient mariners performed their voyages have not yet died out among seafaring men. Every object which meets their gaze is endowed with some miraculous agency for good or for evil. The superstitions of bygone ages, of pagan antiquity and of Christian medievalism, are not yet extinct among the seafaring communities of our own days and have only been modified. Thus the particular seasons of the year, the days of the week, certain encounters of men, women and animals, are still regarded with superstitious fancy by sailors and fishermen. They firmly believe in omens which either warn them of danger or augur luck and success.

The encounter of certain persons is said to predict ill-luck when the seafaring man is about to set out on a voyage. Curiously enough, mariners seem to have a certain antipathy for lawyers, " landshark " being a term applied to gowned men. Among some sailors the disfavour is extended to tailors. Thus in Morbihan to meet a tailor, or dressmaker, is considered a bad sign, and one has to be careful not to pronounce their names in the presence of one who is going out to sea.[1]

The ban, however, lies particularly heavy on priests, who are synonymous with Jonah among seafaring men. Priests are feared most of all, no doubt, on account of their black dress and their office of burying the dead. It is not only unlucky to have a

---

[1] *Revue des Traditions populaires*, Vol. VI, p. 541.

THE FISHERMAN'S FAMILY
by Puvis de Chavannes

priest at sea, but even to speak to one or to meet
him on shore before embarking upon a sea-voyage.
During the Middle Ages priests were even credited
with the power of raising storms. The superstition
attaching to priests is very widespread and exists
among English, Scottish, French, Swedish, and
even Japanese sailors and especially fishermen.
Thus when at sea some Scottish fishermen never pronounced the words " minister," " kirk," " salmon,"
" swine," and " dog." A minister in a boat at sea
was looked upon with much misgiving. He might
be another Jonah. The minister was called at sea
" the man wi' the black quyte," and the kirk, " the
bell-hoose."[1]

An amusing story is told in *Notes znd Queries*,
illustrating the reluctance of seamen to mention the
words " salmon," " sow," and " minister." Once
a fishing-boat left Moray Firth, having on board
six men and a boy who was fond of jokes. Perceiving an empty salmon tin floating on the water,
the lad turned to the fishermen and said : " Here
is an empty salmon tin which would make an
excellent trough for our minister's sow ! " The
horrified crew would have thrown the rascal into
the water had not his father, the owner of the boat,
interfered.[2]

The ill-favour attached to priests is shared by
women. If Firth of Forth fishermen meet a bare-

[1] See Gregor, *Folklore of Scotland*, p. 199.
[2] Mélusine, Vol. II, col. 235.

footed woman with flat feet when they are pro-
ceeding to the sea, they are sure of having bad luck
on that day and prefer to stay at home.   A Cornish
fisherman maintained that every morning he met
a woman who wished him good luck, but he never
had any.[1]   In Sweden fishermen pretend that if a
woman steps over the rod then no trout will be
caught on that day.[2]   The idea that women are
unlucky at sea is particularly strong among French
sailors.   Thus the mariners of Finistère pretend
that at St. Jean du Dight the sea grows angry at
the sight of a woman.   In this respect the ancients
were much more gallant, for we read in Pliny's
Natural History that if a woman appears naked
before the winds they immediately subside.[3]   In
the neighbourhood of Paimpol, and in Brittany,
it is considered unlucky by the fishermen to meet a
Sister of Mercy or an old maid.

Some Scottish fishermen will not go to sea if a
lame man crosses their path, and in the neighbourhood of Aberdeen it is considered unlucky to meet
a red-haired or flat-footed person.

Among men belonging to different nationalities
Finns and Laplanders seem to loom particularly
large in the imagination of sailors.   They are
supposed to be able to raise winds and storms and
to do all sorts of uncanny things.   It is therefore

[1] Sébillot, *Le Folklore des Pêcheurs*, p. 184.
[2] See Jones, *Credulities, past and present*, p. 116.
[3] Vol. XXVIII.

dangerous to have them on board of ship. Even
certain family names are supposed to be unlucky
among some seafaring men and particularly fishermen. Thus some Scottish fishermen will not meet
or even pronounce the names of *Ross*, *Coull*, and
Whyte when going to sea.[1]

Priests and women, however, are not the only
harbingers of ill-luck among seafaring men, for the
ill-favour is shared by certain animals. Among the
animals of evil augury, unlucky visitors on board
of ship, who are particularly prominent in the
imagination of sailors and fishermen are : hares,
pigs, cats, and sometimes also dogs, horses, and
spiders. English and Scottish mariners and fishermen consider it unlucky so much as to mention a
four-footed animal at sea. " The men of several of
the villages would not pronounce the word *swine*
when at sea."[2] A hare crossing the path portended
mishap on the journey. Even so much as to talk of
hares is an ominous sign to the fishermen of Cornwall, as the beginning of a voyage on Candlemas Day
is to mariners.[3] The superstition connected with
cats is widespread in Brittany and Morbihan. On
the other hand, the presence of rats in a ship is
considered to be a good sign and it indicates misfortune if they leave the vessel.

[1] See Gregor, l.c., p. 201.
[2] Gregor, l.c., p. 129.
[3] See Jones, l.c., p. 116 ; Gregor, l.c., p. 129 ; W. Henderson,
Notes on Folklore, p. 204.

One of the superstitions which still cling to sea-faring people is the belief in lucky and unlucky days. There are supposed to be twenty-eight lucky days which the angel Gabriel revealed to St. Joseph, while fifty-four days are exceedingly unlucky when no sea-journey should be undertaken. Among the unlucky days are the first Monday in April, the birthday of Cain and the day on which Abel was slain; the second Monday in August, which is supposed to be the anniversary of the destruction of Sodom and Gomorrah. The thirty-first of December is also unlucky, because Judas, who betrayed the Saviour, hanged himself on that day. He who goes out fishing on this day will catch no fish, but bones of a corpse and a shroud. Candlemas Day is supposed to be ill-omened for sailing.

Among the days of the week Saturday is some-times considered inauspicious and sometimes, on the contrary, fortunate. But the day which is regarded with superstitious fancies not only by seafaring individuals, but also by many landsmen, is Friday. " Friday," writes Gregor, " was specially avoided as the day on which to begin any piece of work. It was very unlucky for a ship to sail on this day."[1] There is a popular superstition that on Friday the witches and the nixies reign supreme and wield great power over the waters. When the King of Poland was in Danzig in 1533 and, holding Mon-

[1] Gregor, *Folklore of North-East of Scotland*, p. 149.

day and Friday as unlucky days, refused to sail on them, he very frequently missed favourable winds.

" Many a good ship," writes Southey, " lost that tide which might have led to fortune, because the captain and the crew thought it unlucky to begin their voyage on Friday." If it were possible for the captain to devise some excuse for remaining till the morrow, he was sure to postpone his journey.

The superstition which makes the seaman dread Friday as an ominous day has been attributed to its connection with the Crucifixion. It is, however, quite possible that the seaman has inherited the superstition from pagan days, for the dread of Friday is not at all limited to Christians. Friday derived its name from Freya or Frigga, the wife of Odin. She was thought to be the mother of all the pagan divinities of the northern nations begotten by Odin. For pagan antiquity Frigga was the representative of the Eternal Feminine, and for that very reason triumphant Christianity deprived her of her halo, pointing out the shady side of her nature, placing in her stead the Stella Maris. As long as Frigga or Freya held her sway in pagan antiquity there is no trace of the superstition, Friday, on the contrary, being considered as one of the luckiest days. It is only five centuries after the introduction of Christianity among the northern nations that the superstition concerning Friday appears.

Numerous are the folk-tales and legends current among seafaring people illustrating the superstition that Friday is a black day for sailing. The *Wellesley*, leaving for the West Indies, got under way on Friday the 24th of March, 1848, but was recalled by the Port Admiral and did not leave again until the following day. The ship's crew firmly believed that the admiral had purposely left something behind so as to avoid going to sea on Friday.[1]

Lord Byron, who shared all the superstitions of the Highlanders, held Friday to be an unlucky day, but he nevertheless embarked on this ill-omened day for Greece and died at Missolonghi.

The superstition concerning Friday is still very strong among seafaring people, and there are many marine officers, although themselves above super- stition, who will categorically refuse to sail on Friday. The reason is very simple. They know that the crew will still be clinging to the old super- stition and in the event of a gale, or any other mishap, they will be demoralized and lose courage, accepting the threatening danger as something unavoidable. "What is the good of trying to fight against fate," they will think, "when we are doomed to destruction, having set sail on a Friday?"

The British Admiralty once tried to prove the absurdity of this superstition. It caused the keel of a ship to be laid on Friday, named her Friday, and

[1] See Jones, l.c., p. 109.

launched her on a Friday. It gave the command to a captain whose name was Friday. The ship commenced her first voyage on a Friday. Although it was a well-appointed vessel when it left port, neither ship nor crew was ever heard of.[1]

Pomeranian sailors consider it lucky to employ a piece of stolen timber at the building of a vessel; at night such a ship is supposed to run smoothly over the water. It is lucky for a ship to have an old coin hidden under the mast. Salt is supposed to bring luck to seafaring people. The spilling of salt on the table is almost universally considered as a bad omen, but to carry salt in one's pocket is supposed by sailors and fishermen to bring luck. In 1700 no fisherman of the Isle of Man would go out fishing without carrying some salt in his pocket, and towards the end of last century they were still in the habit of throwing some salt into the sea.

The old shoe and the horseshoe are not particular superstitions of sailors.

If a fly fell into a glass out of which anyone had been drinking or was about to drink, fishermen of Greenock looked upon it as a good omen.

The superstitious belief attached to a child's caul is of course well known. It is not only supposed among many nations to bring luck to the child itself,

[1] See Mélusine, Vol. II, col. 233; Ralston, *Russian Folk-tales*, p. 199.

but to preserve the man who possessed it from drowning. It used to be frequently advertised for sale in the newspapers, and fetched as much as twenty guineas.

The caul was and still is supposed by superstitious sailors to have the power of preserving them from drowning. The price, however, seems to have come down. Thus, while former sellers used to ask, and probably obtain, fifteen, twenty and even thirty guineas for a child's caul, some were offered towards the end of last century for thirty shillings. This superstition which has been traced to remote antiquity was very prevalent in the primitive ages of the Church, and several Fathers of the Church inveighed against it. The superstition exists among many nations, and proverbs in French, German, and Yiddish point to it. " To be born in a little shirt," say the Jews in Russia and Poland, while the French proverb, " être né coiffé," is a well-known expression and is referred to in *Gil Blas*.

We have spoken above of the fear of sailors and fishermen to carry priests or lawyers on board, and of their objection to name certain objects. It is also considered unlucky by fishermen to be numbered when either standing or walking. To be spoken to by someone while on his way to the boats is considered a bad omen. Swedish fishermen share this belief with their comrades in England and at St. Malo. A Scotch fisherman will give the indiscreet enquirer whither he was going a rather rude answer. " May the devil tear out your tongue."

The fisherman is firmly convinced that if someone speaks to him or even wishes him good luck he is sure not to catch any fish. In Portessie fishermen even went so far as to beat the enquirer and to " draw blood," so as turn the ill-luck.[1] The superstition that anyone saying good-luck is ominous exists in Scotland, Sweden, and France.[2] Breton fishermen even believe that if one looks at them very hard it is ominous.

Among the bad omens is the loss of either a water-bucket or a mop at sea. To play cards on board is considered unlucky by seamen, while sneezing depends upon what side it has taken place. To sneeze on the right side, at the moment of embarking, betokens a favourable voyage, while a sneeze on the left side is a decidedly bad omen. To lose the flag is a bad omen and particularly to hand it to another sailor through the rungs of a ladder. Children on board ship bring good luck, but cats are unlucky.

American sailors will never start on a voyage unless there is a mascot on board. Sea-captains are tempted to go back to harbour if they see a bird fly across the ship. A swab or a bucket lost over-

[1] See Gregor, *Folklore,* p. 199; *Folklore Journal,* Vol. IV, p. 12.

[2] See *Revue des Traditions populaires,* Vol. VI, p. 117; Vol. IX, p. 119; *Folklore Journal,* Vol. VII, p. 45.

board fills the sailor with foreboding, while the accidental tearing of a flag and mending it on the quarter-deck is considered to be most unlucky. The old-fashioned black travelling bags are taboo for sailors or, at least, were so in the past. Formerly sailors believed that all black things on board ship were omens of ill.[1]

One often hears old salts say, when they hear of a ship lost, " Aye, I always knew she would never come to port ; I knew she were bound to Davy Jones." There are ships which in the belief of sailors are doomed to be unlucky. They may have been launched on a " black day," or by someone sure to bring ill-luck. Her keel was laid on an unlucky day or may have been built on an unlucky slip.

Bells play a part in sailors' superstitions. The lonely fisherman in the Baltic Sea still pretends that he can hear the sound of the bells of Vineta, and the fishermen of Normandy listens for the muffled sound of the bells of Jersey. It happened during a long civil war, when the State was short of money. The bells in the churches of Jersey were consequently collected and sent to France to be turned into coin of the realm. During the passage a storm arose and the ship foundered. When a gale is coming these bells are supposed to ring, and if the fisherman can hear their sound

[1] See *Memoirs of the American Folklore Society*, 1925, Vol. XVIII.

before embarking nothing will induce him to leave.

There is a story of a bell on the grave of a sea-captain in the cemetery of St. Leven, in Cornwall, which strikes the half-hour. If, however, someone approaches the grave for the purpose of listening to the bell he is sure to meet with misfortune. One day a seaman heard eight bells strike and soon afterwards he died.[1]

One day the bell of a sinking ship is said to have begun to ring by itself. A legend from Helgoland also relates that one day, no one knew whence, a bell upon a crucifix was driven on shore by an easterly gale. Whenever afterwards an east wind was required it was sufficient to pray before the crucifix and to ring the bell to obtain such a wind.[2]

Another legend relates that once a boat, manned by a piratical crew, entered Nijkerk in Holland. The pirates possessed themselves of the silver bell and conveyed it to their boat. But no sooner had the pirates left the shore when a violent storm arose and the boat with the pirates foundered.[3] A similar legend is related of St. Goven's bell. Here the bell was borne away and entombed in a stone on the brink of the wall. When the stone is struck, the silver tones of the bell are heard.

[1] Bottrell, *Traditions of Cornwall*, p. 477.
[2] See Heims, *Seespuck*, p. 70.
[3] See Heims, l.c., p. 69.

There is also a tale of the Kentsham bell which sunk away in the depths of the sea because the captain of the vessel carrying it had sworn an oath.[1] Some sailors believe that the demons of the sea are frightened when they hear the sound of bells. A similar superstition exists in Ireland where people believe that the ringing of bells keeps away evil spirits.[2] There is a custom prevailing at Malta to ring the bells for an hour during a gale, so that the winds may cease and the sea be calmed. A similar custom exists also in France, in Tuscany, in Sicily, and in Sardinia.

The ceremony of christening a ship can be traced to antiquity, when vessels were placed under the protection of particular pagan gods, and libations were practised when the vessel was launched. At present Catholic sailors are convinced that a ship that has not been christened is much more exposed to danger than are those which have been. In 1880 it happened that a fisherman at St. Malo caught but little fish and his ill-luck was attributed to the fact that his boat had not been christened. The owner of a boat which has not been baptised, fishermen say, is sure to be drowned. In Brittany it would be difficult to find a crew for a vessel which has not been christened.[3] The ceremony accompanying the christening of vessels in Brittany is

[1] See *Folklore Journal*, 1884, p. 21.
[2] See *Folklore Record*, Vol. IV, p. 99.
[3] See Sébillot, *Folklore des Pêcheurs*, 1901, p. 141.

rather picturesque. Biscuits are crushed on deck
and a bottle of wine is broken on the prow, the owner
reciting the lines :

> " Biscuit et bouteille de vin,
> Fais que sur mon bateau ne manque
> Jamais du pain."

The godfather and godmother of the vessel then
bend down, gather up the crumbs of the biscuits
and lick up the wine. The godfather is addressed
as wood-godfather, and the godmother as wood-
godmother, as it is wood they have christened
and not a human being.[1]

In Scotland a boat was launched to a flowing tide,
sometimes prow foremost and sometimes stern
foremost. When the boat was in the water, whisky
in free quantity and bread and cheese were distributed among those present at the launch. The
boat was then named, and a bottle containing
whisky was broken on the prow or stern, according
to the way the boat had been launched. The
following words were spoken before breaking the
bottle :

> " Fae rocks an saands
> An barren lands
> Anill men's hands
> Keep's free
> Aeel oot, weel in
> Wi a gueede shot."

GREGOR, *Folklore of North-East of Scotland*, p. 197.

In Japan there seems to exist the custom, instead

[1] Sébillot, l.c., p. 143.

of breaking a bottle of champagne, when a ship is launched, to let loose hundreds of turtle-doves.[1]

The custom of blessing a ship already existed in the fourteenth century. The Bishop of Bangor received five pounds for his expenses to go to Southampton to bless the king's ship, *Henri Grace de Dieu*. Columbus and his companions went in solemn procession to the cloister La Rabida, where they spent the night in prayers.[2]

In Brittany, when a vessel going out for the first time has been damaged, it is not put to sea again before at least a week.[3]   In Scotland a boat which had been wrecked with the loss of life and cast ashore was allowed to lie and go to pieces. No fisherman of the village to which it belonged would have set foot in it to put to sea, or carry away a board as firewood.[4]

Altogether, sailors and fishermen still cling to the superstition that it is unlucky to break up an old boat, and this superstition accounts for the reason why a good many useless boats are seen in fishing villages.

It is supposed to be unlucky to wear the clothes of a fellow-sailor who has died at sea before the termination of the voyage.[5]

There was an old superstition among sailors,

[1] Mélusine, Vol. III, col. 239.
[2] See Heims, l.c., p. 151.
[3] Sébillot, *Folklore des Pêcheurs*, p. 148.
[4] See Gregor, l.c., p. 198.
[5] Grant, l.c., p. 399.

and it is supposed still to linger among them, that the total loss or tearing of a ship's colours would be followed by a great calamity. The sails split, the spars carried away, or the masts gone by the board, are not supposed to be such misfortunes as that of being deprived of the colours. The loss or tearing of a flag was, and still is, a sure sign of misfortune, both to the vessel and the crew.[1]

[1] Grant, l.c., p. 385.

SUPERSTITIONS OF SAILORS IN
ENGLISH LITERATURE

CHAPTER XII

SUPERSTITIONS OF SAILORS IN ENGLISH LITERATURE

Allusions to seamen's superstitions—Drayton, Longfellow and Dryden—Sir Walter Scott and Dickens—Shakespeare—Death and the rising tide—Falstaff's death—Peggotty on Barkis's death—St. Elmo's light—Allusions in *The Tempest*—Thomas Heyrick's *Submarine Voyage*—The sale of winds—Sumner's *Last Will and Testament*—Michael Drayton's lines in *The Moon-Calf*—mermen and mermaids—Old English Ballads—*The Master of Weemys*—A poem by Leyden—allusions by Shakespeare—The barnacle goose—Marston's *Malcontent*—Butler's *Hudibras*—Michael Drayton's *Polyolbion*—allusion to barnacle goose in *The Tempest*—A corpse on board—Walter Scott's *Pirate*—Lucky and unlucky days—An old proverb—Shakespeare's allusions to lucky days—" 'Tis a lucky day, boy."

COPIOUS allusions to the many superstitions of seamen described in the preceding chapters abound in English and Continental literature. The authors and poets seem to have been thoroughly acquainted with the superstitions prevailing among their contemporaries. Numerous allusions are found in Old English Ballads, in the poems of Drayton, Longfellow, and Dryden, in the works of Sir Walter Scott, and Dickens, and in the plays of Shakespeare. We have collected a few which will illustrate this statement.

The superstition of seamen as well as of landsmen

that no man could die with the rising tide and that
death was delayed until the ebb, is alluded to by
Shakespeare and Dickens. Thus Mrs. Quickly,
when speaking of Falstaff's death, says :

" 'A made a finer end, and went away, an it had
been any christom child ; 'a parted even just between twelve and one, e'en at the turning o' the
tide."[1]

The passage referring to Barkis's death in *David
Copperfield* is well known. " People," said Mr.
Peggotty the fisherman, " can't die along the coast
except when the tide is pretty nigh out. They
can't be born unless it's pretty nigh in—not properly
born till flood. He's agoing out with the tide—he's
agoing out with the tide. It's ebb at half-arter
three, slack-water half-an-hour. If he lives till it
turns he'll hold his own till past the flood, and go
out with the next tide."[2]

St. Elmo's light, or Castor and Pollux, and the
superstitions connected with this phenomenon which
we have described in Chapter II, is alluded to in
The Tempest, when Ariel says :

" On the topmast,
    The yards and bowsprits, would I flame distinctly."[3]

Among the numerous other references to St.

[1] *Henry V*, II, 3.
[2] Dickens, *David Copperfield ;* see also Henderson, *Folklore
of the Northern Counties*, p. 58.
[3] *The Tempest*, I, 2.

Elmo's light the following occurs in the *Submarine Voyage*, by Thomas Heyrick :

> " For lo ! a sudden storm did rend the air :
> The sullen Heaven, curling in frowns its brow,
> Did dire presaging omens show ;
> Ill-boding Helena alone was there."[1]

The superstition of sailors that witches could produce winds and storms and that sorcerers were able to sell favourable winds is alluded to in Sumner's *Last Will and Testament* :

> " In Ireland and in Denmark both,
> Witches for gold will sell a man a wind,
> Which, in the corner of a napkin wrapp'd,
> Shall blow him safe unto what coast he will."

Michael Drayton refers to the belief that witches could sell winds in the following lines :

> " She could sell winds to any one that would
> Buy them for money, forcing them to hold
> What time she listed, tie them in a thread,
> Which ever as the seafarer undid,
> They rose or scantled, as his sails would drive,
> To the same port whereas he would arrive."[2]

The numerous superstitions connected with mermen and mermaids and their legendary existence are described in several Old English Ballads :

> " And shee kembit her haire and aye shee sang
> As she festerit on the foam
> And shee gliskit about and round about
> Upon the waters wan.
> O nevir again on land or sea

[1] *Submarine Voyage*, 1691, 2. See also W. C. Hazlitt, *Faiths and Folklore*. s.v., Castor and Pollux.
[2] The works of Michael Drayton, 1753, Vol. II, p. 499, *The Moon-Calf*.

Shall be seen suk a fair woman
And shee shed the haire off her milk white bree
Wi' her finger sae sma' and lang
Sae louder was aye her sang.
As she rade upon the sea,
If ye bee men of Christian moulde
Throwe the master out to me.
It's never a word spake the master baulde,
But a loud laugh leuch the crewe,
And in the deep then the mermayden
Down drappit frae their viewe."[1]

This superstition has been illustrated by Leyden,
in the poem quoted above (Chapter VII), and
references to it are also made by Shakespeare.
Thus Oberon speaks of " a mermaid on a dolphin's
back,"[2] while in 3 *Henry VI*, the line occurs :

" I will drown more sailors than the mermaid shall."[3]

and

" O train me not, sweet mermaid, with thy note."[4]

" A seeming mermaid steers at the helm "
(*Anthony and Cleopatra*, II, 2) are other passages
alluding to the legendary existence of mermaids.

Another well-known superstition among seamen
that it is unlucky to have a corpse on board is
alluded to by Shakespeare, when the sailor says to
Pericles :

" Sir, your queen must overboard : the sea works

---

[1] Motherwell, *The Master of Weemys ;* see *Illustrations of
Northern Antiquities*, 1814 ; see also *Folklore Record*, 1879, Vol. II,
p. 104.
[2] *Midsummer Night's Dream*, II, 1.
[3] *Henry VI*, III, 2.
[4] *Comedy of Errors*, III, 2.

high, the wind is loud, and will not lie till the ship be cleared of the dead ! "[1]

We have mentioned in Chapter IX the curious belief connected with the barnacle goose. Now this belief is alluded to by Marston, when he writes :

> " Like your Scotch barnacle, now a block,
> Instantly a worm, and presently a great goose."
>
> MARSTON, *The Malcontent.*

It is mentioned by Butler in *Hudibras* (III, 2), and described by Drayton in his *Polyolbion :*

> " Whereas those scatter'd trees, which naturally partake
> The fatness of the soil (in many a slimy lake
> Their roots so deeply soak'd) send from their stocky boughs
> A soft and sappy grim, from which those tree-geese grow,
> Call'd barnacles by us, which like a jelly first
> To the beholder seem, then by the fluxure nurs'd,
> Still great and greater thrive, until you well may say
> Them turn'd to perfect fowls, when droping from the tree
> Into the merey pond, which under them doth lie
> Wax ripe, and taking wing, away in flocks do fly ;
> Which well our ancients did among our wonders place."[2]

The allusion to the barnacle goose by Shakespeare is found in *The Tempest :*

> " We shall lose our time,
> And all be turn'd to barnacles."[3]

Among the superstitions of seamen described in the preceding chapters we have mentioned their

---

[1] *Pericles,* III, 1.

[2] Drayton, the works of, Vol. III, p. 119P, *Polyolbion*, Song 27 ; see also Hazlitt, *Faiths and Folklore,* s.v. ; J. E. Harting, *The Ornithology of Shakespeare,* 1871, p. 246 ; Nares, *Glossary,* 1822, s.v., p. 29.

[3] *Tempest,* IV, 1.

reluctance to save a person from drowning. We have quoted a passage from Sir Walter Scott's *Pirate*, and there is also an allusion to it in Shakespeare.[1]

The belief of seamen in lucky and unlucky days is almost a general superstition and is frequently alluded to in literature.[2]

There is an old proverb which seems to illustrate the seaman's dread of Friday :

> " Friday's moon
> Come when it will, it comes too soon."

Shakespeare alludes to the superstition in *King John* (III, 1), in *Macbeth* (IV, 1, and in *A Winter's Tale* (III, 3).

> " 'Tis a lucky day, boy ; and
> W'ill do good deeds on't."

[1] *Twelfth Night.*
[2] See Hazlitt, l.c., s.v., and J. Aubrey, *Miscellanies*, 1857, p. l. ff.

THE END

BIBLIOGRAPHY

In addition to the works quoted in the footnotes the following books have been consulted for the compilation of the present volume.

Balleydier, A., *Veillées maritimes*. Paris, 1854.

Bassett, F. S., *Legends and Traditions of the Sea and Sailors*. London, 1885.

Bassett, W., *Wanderships*. Chicago, 1917.

Bosquet, A., *La Normandie Romanesque et merveilleuse*. Paris, 1845.

Bottrell, W., *Traditions and Hearthside Stories of West Cornwall*. 1870.

Cunningham, A., *Traditional Tales of the English and Scottish Peasantry*. London, 1822.

Dasent, Sir G. W., *Popular Tales from the Norse*. Edinburgh, 1888.

Gervasus von Tilbury, *Otia Imperialia*. Ed. F. Liebrecht, Hanover, 1856.

Gregor, Rev. W., *Notes on the Folklore of the North-east of Scotland*. London, 1881.

Heims, P. G., *Seespuk, Aberglauben, Märchen und Schnurren*. Leipsic, 1888.

Jal, A., *Scènes de la vie maritime*. Paris, 1830.

Kuhn, A., and W. Schwartz, *Nord deutsche Sagen, Märchen und Gebräuche*. Leipsic, 1848.

Log Book, The, or *Nautical Miscellany*. London, 1830.

Procopius, *De bello gothico*. Leipsic, 1905.

Schmidt, H., *Seemanns-Sagen und Schiffer Märchen*. 1845.

Sébillot, P., *Le Folk-Lore des Pêcheurs*. Paris, 1901.

Thorpe, B., *Northern Mythology*. London, 1852.

Wright, T., *The Voyage of St. Brandan*. Publications of the Percy Society.

PERIODICALS AND REVIEWS

Am Urquell.
Ausland.
Folk-lore Journal. London.
Folk-lore Record. London.
Germania.
Journal of American Folklore.
Mélusine. Paris.
Revue des Traditions Populaires. Paris.

INDEX

A

Agnes Sampson, 80
Al Samiri, 225
Animals, cause of tempests, 83
Anten, lake of, 199
Apple, the, from Tree of Life, 119
Avenging wave, the, 197

B

Ballads, Old English, 277
Bakarra, 20
Barnacle, the, 216, 279
Batarra Gourou, 20
Bathing in sea, 43
Bay, the, of the Departed, 242
Bells, superstitions connected with, 266
Berbido, city of, 149
Bernard Fokke, 233
Bhahgirata, 19
Blaster, 68
Blessing of ships, 270
Bornholm, isle of, origin, 238
Bottreux, bells of the Squire of, 74
Brasi, the, 51
Brooms, and favourable winds, 92
Byron, Lord, superstitions of, 262

C

Cards, playing of, 265
Cask, burning, 241
Cat, christened, 81
Cats, superstitions connected with, 259
Caul, child's, 263
Christening of ship, 268
Christiansö, isle of, origin, 238
Cities, submerged, 147
"Cohulfeen drinth," 198
Coins, old, superstition connected with, 263
Collrus, the lady of, 198
Conches, 71
Cosmogonies, ancient, 16
Creation, story of, 17

D

Dahut, Princess, 48
Davy Jones, 142
Days, lucky and unlucky, 260, 280
Dead, island of the, 132
Demons, of the sea, 239
Dermat o' Dyna, 144
Devil ships, 270
Dickens, superstitions in works of, 276
Drew, the, 208
Drowning men, 239
Drowning Stol, the, 137

283

E

Enderle of Ketch, 243

F

Falkenberg, 226
Family names, 259
Fincara, island of, 143
Finlaps, sorcerers, 97
Finns, 258
Fiolnir, 23
Fish, feel the weather, 70
Flying, the, Dutchman, 225
Fokke, Bernard, 233
Folk medicine, 31
Folk-tales, in *Talmud*, 211
Fox, and angel of death, 58
Friday, unlucky day, 260, 280
Frodi, King, 23

G

Gargantua, 236
Ghost stories, 243
Giant ships, 236
Grallon, King, 147
Grande Chasse Fondre, 236
Grottasavngr, 24
Grotti, 24
Guinunga-gap, 19
Gummer's ore, 129, 209
Gunnar's stone, 199
Gurri, 134
Gustr, 68
Gylf, King, 128

H

Hafgufa, the, 206
Harlem, seawoman of, 194

Hawai, island, origin of, 127
Hiawatha, song of, 67
" Hudibras," superstition mentioned in, 279

I

Is, city of, 147
Island, of the dead, 132
Islands, floating, 126
Islands, inhabited by women, 130
Islands, vanishing, 208
Isle of Man, origin of, 150

J

Jack Harry's lights, 58, 234
Jack with a lantern, 54
Jersey, bells of, 266
Jew, the wandering, 225
Jupille, the mermaids of, 186

K

Kelpies, 178
Kentsham bell, the, 268
Kraken, the, 205
Kunnan, isle of, 134

L

Lapland, sorcerers of, 86, 258
Lawyers, superstition connected with, 256
Leviathan, the, 52, 159, 211
Loholm, castle of, 199

Lucky days, 260
Luonnotar, 19, 133
Lyonesse, the lost, 147

M

Macingo, the, 67
Maga-Kami, 39
Magellan, voyage of, 55
Maildun, the hero, 143, 145
Man, isle of, 150
Manabozho, 67
Manningfual, 236
Margyzr, 167
Marmaete, 174
Marston, superstitions mentioned in works of, 279
Merman, the, and the fisherman's daughter, 189
Mermaid, the, poem by Leyden, 177
Mermaids, love of music, 165; anxious to acquire a soul, 166; sealskins of, 192; lack of soul, 195; Rock of the, 202
Mermen, superstitions about, 164
Milham, bird, 158
Mill, the magic, 23 33, 51
Mill Song, the, 23
Moenslnit, 134
Mother Carey's chickens, 71
Mountains, magnetic, 137
Moyatos, Jean, 244

N

Nagapagoha, 20
Neck, mischievous spirit, 43

North, Captain, 68, 111
North wind, the, 110

O

Oho-Magatshi, 39
Ortach, rock of, 136

P

Paro-el-Bahri, 153
Petrel, the stormy, 71
Phantom ships, 222
Pile of Foulders, 216
Polyolbion, superstitions mentioned in, 279
Pontoppidan, on Kraken, 208; on mermaids, 168
Porpoises, in stormy weather, 70
Priests, cause of tempests, 77, 256

Q

Quern, the magic, 25

R

Rabbi bar bar Hanah, tales, of, 211
Rana, goddess, 33
Rocks, origin of, 132
Rote of waves, 34
Ronge-gorge, 149
Rousalki, 190

S

Sadko, the Novgorod trader, 190
Samiri, al, 225
Sampson, Agnes, 80
Sandflossen, 129
Sandgranis, the, 22
Saturday, superstitions, connected with, 260
Saint Brandanus, 210
Saint Christopher, 60
St. Elmo, lights of, 53, 59, 240
Saint Goven's bell, 267
Saundersfoot, the mermaid of, 202
Sea, arrogance of, 21 ; daughter of the gods, 18 ; divinity, 18 ; origin of, 18 ; demons of the, 239 ; maiden of the, 200
Sea-mischief, 209
Sea-monsters, 211
Sea-water, 30, 32 ; salty taste of, 20
Sea-woman, of Harlem, 194
Seeland, island of, 128
Sewing, at sea, 93
Shakespeare, superstitions mentioned in works of, 276
Ships, christening of, 268
Sleipnir, Norse, 66
Sneezing, at sea, 265
Sol-draulen, the, 209
Solomon, King, power over wind, 106
Souls, in pain, 58
Stella Maris, 261
Storms, 79
Sumner's Last Will, 277
Sun-egg, the, 17

T

Tailors, superstitions connected with, 256

Tairibu, 105
Talmud, folk-tales in, 211
Tannin, the, 48
Tempests, due to demons, 76
Three waves, story of the, 35
Tide, the, 38 ; Plato's view on, 39
Til-fa-toun, 143
Towns, sunken, 148
Tsar Morskoi, 142, 190

U

Universe, origin of, 17

V

Vaisseau phantôme, le, 223
Verdelet, rock of, 135
Vineta, the bells of, 266
Volkhoff, the nymph, 191
Voltigeur, le, 230
Voromatautoru, 105

W

Wainamoinen, 142
Wak, island of, 131
Wandering Jew, the, 225
Waters, arrogance of, 20 ; priority of, 17
Waterspouts, 47 ; origin of, 50
Wave, the avenging, 197 ; the ninth, 36
Waves, noise of, 33 ; number, 34 ; country beneath, 143 ; men beneath the, 153
Wellamo, origin of, 142
Whale, dimension of, 210
Whirlwind, 67

Whistling, at sea, 89

Wind, raising of, 86 ; presents offered to, 106 ; and charitable woman, 113

Wind knots, 83

Winds, spirit of the, 65 ; demons and giants, 66 ; the Four, 66 ; favourable, 85 ; personification of, 104 ; cave of, 117

Witches, power to raise storms, 79

Women, superstitions connected with, 258

Wood-godfather, 269

Words, superstitions connected with, 257

Wrens, superstitions connected with, 178

Y

Yaco-Magatshi, 39

Ymer, 18